Thomas Secker

Lectures on the Catechism of the Church of England

with a discourse on confirmation 7th ed - Vol. 2

Thomas Secker

Lectures on the Catechism of the Church of England
with a discourse on confirmation 7th ed - Vol. 2

ISBN/EAN: 9783337262297

Printed in Europe, USA, Canada, Australia, Japan

Cover: Foto ©Lupo / pixelio.de

More available books at **www.hansebooks.com**

LECTURES

ON THE

CATECHISM

OF THE

CHURCH of ENGLAND:

WITH A

DISCOURSE

ON

CONFIRMATION.

By THOMAS SECKER, LL.D.
Late Lord Archbishop of Canterbury.

THE SEVENTH EDITION.

Publifhed from the Original Manufcripts
By BEILBY PORTEUS, D.D. and GEORGE STINTON, D.D.
His Grace's Chaplains.

VOL. II.

LONDON:
Printed for J. RIVINGTON and SONS, St. Paul's Church-yard;
and B. WHITE and SON, at Horace's Head, Fleet-ftreet.
M,DCC,XC.

LECTURE XXII.

The Fifth Commandment.

PART I.

HAVING explained the Precepts of the firſt Table, which ſet forth the Duty of Men to God; I now come to thoſe of the Second, which expreſs our ſeveral Obligations one to another.

Now the whole Law, concerning theſe Matters, *is briefly comprehended*, as St. *Paul* very juſtly obſerves, *in this* one *Saying*, *Thou ſhalt love thy Neighbour as thyſelf* [a]. Our Neighbour is every one, with whom we have at any Time any Concern, or on whoſe Welfare our Actions can have any Influence. For whoever is thus within our Reach, is in the moſt important Senſe near to us, however diſtant in other Reſpects. To *love*

[a] Rom. xiii. 9.

our Neighbour, is to bear him Good-will; which of Courſe will diſpoſe us to think favourably of him, and behave properly to him. And to *love him as ourſelves*, is, to have, not only a real, but a ſtrong and active Good-will towards him; with a Tenderneſs for his Intereſts, duly proportioned to that, which we naturally feel for our own. Such a Temper would moſt powerfully reſtrain us from every Thing wrong, and prompt us to every Thing right; and therefore is *the fulfilling of the Law*[b], ſo far as it relates to our mutual Behaviour.

But becauſe, on ſome Occaſions, we may either not ſee, or not confeſs we ſee, what is right, and what otherwiſe; our Saviour hath put the ſame Duty in a Light ſomewhat different, which gives the ſafeſt, and fulleſt, and cleareſt Direction for Practice, that any one Precept can give. *All Things, whatſoever ye would that Men ſhould do unto you, even ſo do ye unto them*[c]. Behaving properly depends on judging truly; and that, in Caſes of any Doubt, depends on hearing with due Attention both Sides. To our

[b] Ver. 10.   [c] Matth. vii. 12.

LECTURE XXII.

own Side we never fail attending. The Rule therefore is, give the other Side the same Advantage, by supposing it your own: and after considering carefully and fairly, what, if it were indeed your own, you should not only desire (for Desires may be unreasonable) but think you had an equitable Claim to, and well-grounded Expectation of, from the other Party, that do in Regard to him. Would we but honestly take this Method, our Mistakes would be so exceeding few, and slight, and innocent, that well might our blessed Lord add, *For this is the Law and the Prophets.*

Yet, after all, there might be Difficulty sometimes, especially to some Persons, in the Application of a Rule so very general. And therefore we have, in the Commandments, the reciprocal Duties of Man to Man branched out into six Particulars: The first of which, contained in the fifth Commandment, relates to the mutual Obligations of Superiors and Inferiors; the rest, to those Points in which all Men are considered as Equals.

It is true, the Precept, now to be explained, mentions only one Kind of Superiors. *Thou shalt honour thy Father and thy Mother*. But the Case of other Superiors is so like that of Fathers, that most of them have occasionally the very Name of Father given them in most Languages; and therefore the Regard, due to them also, may be very properly comprehended, and laid before you, under the same Head. It is likewise true, that the Duty of the Inferior alone is expressed in the Commandment; but the corresponding Duty of the Superior is, at the same Time, of Necessity implied: For which Reason I shall discourse of both; beginning with the mutual Obligations of Children and Parents, properly so called, which will be a sufficient Employment for the present Time.

Now the Duty of Children to their Parents is here expressed by the Word *Honour*, which in common Language signifies a Mixture of Love and Respect, producing due Obedience; but in Scripture Language it implies further, Maintenance and Support, when wanted.

1. Love

LECTURE XXII.

1. Love to thofe, of whofe Flefh and Blood we are, is what Nature dictates to us, in the very firft Place. Children have not only received from their Parents, as Inftruments in the Hand of God, the Original of their Being; but the Prefervation of it through all the Years of helplefs Infancy; when the needful Care of them gave much Trouble, took up much Time, and required much Expence; all which, Parents ufually go through, with fo cheerful a Diligence, and fo felf-denying a Tendernefs, that no Return of Affection on the Children's Part can poffibly repay it to the full; though Children's Affection is what, above all Things, makes Parents happy. Then, as Life goes on, it is their Parents that give or procure for them fuch Inftruction of all Kinds, as qualifies them, both to do well in this World, and be for ever bleffed in another; that watch over them continually with never-ceafing Attention, confulting their Inclinations in a Multitude of obliging Inftances, and bearing with their Perverfenefs in a Multitude of provoking ones; kindly reftraining them from a thoufand

nicious Follies, into which they would otherwise fall; and directing their heedless Footsteps into the right Way; encouraging, rewarding, and, which indeed is no less a Benefit, correcting them also, as the Case requires; full of Solicitude all the while for their Happiness, and consuming themselves with Labour and Thoughtfulness for these dear Objects, to improve, support, and advance them in their Lives, and provide for them at their Deaths. Even those Parents, who perform these Duties but imperfectly, who perhaps do some very wrong Things, do notwithstanding, almost all of them, so many right and meritorious ones; that though, the more such they do, the better they should be loved; yet they that do least, do enough to be loved sincerely for it, as long as they live[d].

2. And with Love must ever be joined, secondly, due Respect, inward and outward. For Parents, are not only the Benefactors, but in Rank the Betters, and in Right the Governors, of their Children; whose Dependance is upon them, in Point of Interest,

[d] See Xenophon's Memoirs of Socrates, l. 2. c. 2.

generally; in Point of Duty, always. They ought therefore to think of them with great Reverence, and treat them with every Mark of Submiſſion, in Geſture, in Speech, in the whole of their Behaviour, which the Practice of wife and good Perſons hath eſtabliſhed, as proper Inſtances of filial Regard. And though the Parents be mean in Station, or low in Underſtanding, ſtill the Relation continues, and the Duty that belongs to it. Nay, ſuppoſe they be faulty in ſome Part of their Conduct or Character, yet Children ſhould be very backward to fee this; and it can very ſeldom be allowable for them to ſhew that they ſee it. From the World they ſhould always conceal it, as far as they can; for it is ſhocking beyond Meaſure in *them* to publiſh it. And if ever any Thing of this Nature muſt be mentioned to the Parents themſelves, which nothing but great Neceſſity can warrant or excuſe; it ſhould be with all poſſible Gentleneſs and Modeſty, and the moſt real Concern at being obliged to ſo unnatural an Office.

3. Love

3. Love and Respect to Parents will always produce Obedience to them: a third Duty of the highest Importance. Children, for a considerable Time, are utterly unqualified to govern themselves; and so long as this continues to be the Case, must be absolutely and implicitly governed by those, who alone can claim a Title to it. As they grow up to the Use of Understanding indeed, Reason should be gradually mixed with Authority, in every Thing that is required of them. But at the same Time, Children should observe, what they may easily find to be true in daily Instances, that they are apt to think they know how to direct themselves, much sooner than they really do; and should therefore submit to be directed by their Friends in more Points, and for a longer Time, than perhaps they would naturally be tempted to wish. Suppose, in that Part of your Lives which is already past, you had had your own Way in every Thing, what would have been the Consequences? You yourselves must see, very bad ones. Why other Persons see, what you will see also in time, that it would

LECTURE XXII.

would be full as bad, were you to have your Way now. And what all who are likely to know, agree in, you should believe, and submit to. Your Parents and Governors have at least more knowledge and Experience, if they have not more Capacity, than you. And the Trouble which they take, and the Concern which they feel about you, plainly shew that your Good is the Thing which they have at Heart. The only Reason why they do not indulge you in the Particulars that you wish, is, that they see it would hurt you. And it is a dreadful Venture for you, to think, as yet, of trusting yourselves. Trust therefore to those, whom you have all Manner of Reason to trust: and obey them willingly, who by the Laws of God and Man, have a right to rule you; and, generally speaking, a Power to make you obey at last, be you ever so unwilling.

Not that Children are bound to Obedience in all Things, without Exception. Should a Parent command them to lie, to steal, to commit any Wickedness; God commands the contrary; and He is to be obeyed,

obeyed, not Man. Or should a Parent command any Thing of Consequence, directly opposite to the Laws of the Land, and the Injunctions of public Authority: here the Magistrate, being the superior Power, in all Things that confessedly belong to his Jurisdiction, is to be obeyed, rather than the Parent, who ought himself to be subject to the Magistrate[e]. Or if, in other Points, a Parent should require what was both very evidently, and very greatly, unsuitable to a Child's Condition and Station; or had a clear Tendency to make him miserable; or would be certainly and considerably prejudicial to him through the Remainder of his Life: where the one goes so far beyond his just Bounds, the other may allowably excuse himself from complying. Only the Case must be both so plain, and withal of such a Moment, as may justify him, not only in his own Judgment, which may easily be prejudiced, but in that of every considerate Person, whom he hath Opportunity of consulting, and in the general Opinion of

[e] See Taylor's Elements of Civil Law, p. 387, 388, 389.

Mankind.

LECTURE XXII.

Mankind. And even then, the Refusal must be accompanied with the greatest Decency and Humility; and the strictest Care to make amends, by all Instances of real Duty, for this one seeming Want of Duty.

In Proportion as young Persons approach to that Age, when the Law allows them to be capable of governing themselves, they become by Degrees less and less subject to the Government of their Parents; especially in smaller Matters; for in the more important Concerns of Life, and above all, in the very important one of Marriage, not only Daughters, (concerning whom, the very Phrase of *giving them in Marriage*, shews that they are not to give themselves as they please) but Sons too, should have all possible Regard to the Authority, the Judgment, the Blessing, the Comfort of those, to whom they owe every Thing. And even after they are sent out into the World, to stand on their own Bottom, still they remain for ever bound not to slight, or willingly to grieve them; but in all proper Affairs, to consult with them, and

hearken

hearken to them; as far as it can be at all expected, in Reason or Gratitude, that they should.

4. The last Thing, which in Scripture the Phrase of honouring Parents comprehends, is affording them descent Relief and Support, if they are reduced to want it. For thus our Saviour explains the Word, in his Reproof of the Pharisees, for *making this Commandment of no Effect by their Tradition. God commanded, Honour thy Father and thy Mother: but ye say, whosoever shall say to his Father or Mother, it is a Gift, by whatsoever thou mightest be profited by me*: that is, what should have relieved you, I have devoted to religious Uses: *Whosoever shall say this, and honoureth not his Father or his Mother, he shall be free* [f]. In St. Mark it is, *Ye suffer him no more to do ought for his Father or his Mother* [g]. And in other Places of Scripture, besides this, honouring a Person signifies contributing to his Maintenance: as 1 *Tim.* v. 17, 18. *Let the Elders that rule well, be counted worthy of double Honour: especially they who labour in the*

[f] Matth. xv. 4, 5, 6.   [g] Mark vii. 12.

Word

LECTURE XXII.

Word and Doctrine; for the Scripture faith, the Labourer is worthy of his Reward.

How worthy Parents are of this, as well as the other Sorts of Honour, when they need it, sufficiently appears from all that hath been said. If they deserve to be loved and respected; surely they are not to be left exposed to Distress and Want, by those whom they have brought into Life; and for whom they have done so much: but Children, even if they are poor, should both be diligent in working, and provident in saving, to keep their helpless Parents from Extremities: and if they are in competently good Circumstances, should allow them a liberal Share of the Plenty, which they enjoy themselves. Accordingly St. Paul directs, that both *Children, and Nephews*, that is Grand-children, for so the Word *Nephew* always means in Scripture, should *learn first to shew Piety at Home, and to requite their Parents: for that is good and acceptable before God*[h]. Indeed Nature, as well as Christianity, enjoins it so strongly, that the whole World cries out Shame,

[h] 1 Tim. v. 4.

where

where it is neglected. And the same Reason, which requires Parents to be assisted in their Necessities, requires children also to attend upon them, and minister to them, with vigilant Assiduity and tender Affection, in their Infirmities; and to consult on every Occasion, their Desires, their Peace, their Ease. And they should consider both what they contribute to their Support, and every other Instance of Regard, which they shew them, not as an Alms, given to an Inferior, but as a Tribute of Duty paid to a Superior. For which Reason perhaps it may be, that relieving them is mentioned in Scripture under the Notion of honouring them.

One Thing more to be observed, is, that all these Duties of Children belong equally to both Parents; the Mother being as expresly named, as the Father, in the Commandment; and having the same Right in Point of Reason. Only, if contrary Orders are given by the two Parents to the Child; he is bound to obey that Parent rather, whom the other is bound to obey also: but still preserving to each all due

Reverence

LECTURE XXII.

Reverence: from which nothing, not even the Command of either, can difcharge him[1].

And now I proceed to the Duties of Parents to their Children: on which there is much lefs Need to enlarge, than on the other. For not only Parents have more Underftanding to know their Duty, and ftronger Affections to prompt them to do it: but indeed, a great Part of it hath been already intimated, in fetting forth that of Children to them. It is the Duty of Parents, to take all that kind Care, which is the main Foundation of Love; to keep up fuch Authority, as may fecure Refpect; to give fuch reafonable Commands, as may engage a willing Obedience; and thus to make their Children fo good, and themfelves fo efteemed by them, that they may depend, in cafe of Need, on Affiftance and Succour from them.

More particularly, they are bound to think them, from the firft, worthy of their own Infpection and Pains; and not abandon

---

[1] Pietas Parentibus, etfi inæqualis eft eorum poteftas, æqua debebitur. D. 27. 10. 4.

them to the Negligence, or bad Management of others: so to be tender of them and indulge them, as not to encourage their Faults; so to reprove and correct them, as not to break their Spirits, or provoke their Hatred: to instill into them the Knowledge, and require of them the Practice, of their Duty to God and Man; and recommend to them every Precept, both of Religion and Morality, by what is the strongest Recommendation, a good and amiable Example: to breed them up as suitably to their Condition, as may be; but to be sure not above it; watching over them with all the Care, that conduces to Health; but allowing them in none of the Softness, that produces Luxury or Indolence; or of the needless Distinctions, that pamper Pride: to begin preparing them early, according to their future Station in Life, for being useful in it, to others and themselves: to provide conscientiously for their spiritual and eternal, as well as temporal Good, in disposing of them; and bestow on them willingly, as soon as it is fit, whatever may be requisite to settle them
properly

LECTURE XXII.

properly in the World: to lay up for them not by Injuftice, Penurioufnefs, or immoderate Solicitude, all that they can; but by honeft and prudent Diligence and Attention, as much as is fufficient; and to diftribute this amongft them, not as Fondnefs, or Refentment, or Caprice, or Vanity, may dictate; but in a reafonable and equitable Manner; fuch as will be likelieft to make thofe who receive it, love one another, and efteem the Memory of the Giver.

Thefe are, in brief, the mutual Duties of Parents and Children: and you will eafily perceive that they are the Duties, in Proportion, of all who by any occafional, or accidental Means, come to ftand in the Stead of Parents or of Children. The main Thing which wants to be obferved, is, that from the Neglect of thefe Duties on one Side, or on both, proceeds a very great Part of the Wickednefs and Mifery, that is in the World. May God incline the Hearts of all that are concerned either Way in this moft important Relation, fo to practife the feveral Obligations of it, as may

procure

procure to them, in this World, reciprocal Satisfaction and Joy, and eternal Felicity in that which is to come, through Jesus Christ our Lord!

LECTURE XXIII.

The Fifth Commandment.

PART II.

IN my laſt Diſcourſe I began to explain the fifth Commandment: and having already gone through the Duties of Children and Parents, properly ſo called, I come now to the other Sorts of Inferiors and Superiors: all which have ſometimes the ſame Names given them, and are comprehended under the Reaſon and Equity of this Precept.

And here, the firſt Relation to be mentioned, is, that between private Subjects and thoſe in Authority over them: a Relation ſo very like that of Children and Fathers, that the Duties on both Sides are much the ſame in each.

LECTURE XXIII.

But more particularly, the Duty of Subjects, is, to obey the Laws of whatever Government Providence hath placed us under, in every thing which is not contrary to the Laws of God; and to contribute willingly to its Support, every thing that is legally required, or may be reasonably expected of us: to be faithful and true to the Interests of that Society, of which we are Members; and to the Persons of those, who govern it; paying, both to the supreme Power, and all subordinate Magistrates, every Part of that Submission and Respect, both in Speech and Behaviour, which is their Due; and making all those Allowances in their Favour, which the Difficulty of their Office, and the Frailty of our common Nature, demand: to love and wish well to all our Fellow-Subjects, without Exception; think of them charitably, and treat them kindly; to be peaceable and quiet, each minding diligently the Duties of his own Station; not factious and turbulent, intruding into the Concerns of others: to be modest and humble, *not exercising ourselves in Matters too high for us;*

LECTURE XXIII.

us[a]; but leaving such Things to the Care of our Superiors, and the Providence of God: to be thankful for the Blessings and Advantages of Government, in Proportion as we enjoy them; and reasonable and patient under the Burdens and Inconveniences of it, which at any Time we may suffer.

The Duty of Princes and Magistrates, it would be of little Use to enlarge on at present. In general it is, to confine the Exercise of their Power within the Limits of those Laws, to which they are bound; and direct it to the Attainment of those Ends, for which they were appointed: to execute their proper Function with Care and Integrity, as *Men fearing God, Men of Truth, hating Covetousness*[b]; to do all Persons impartial Justice, and consult, in all Cases, the public Benefit; encouraging Religion and Virtue with Zeal, especially by a good Example; punishing Crimes with Steadiness, yet with Moderation; and *studying to preserve the People committed to their Charge, in Wealth, Peace, and Godliness*[c].

[a] Psalm cxxxi. 1. [b] Exod. xviii. 21. [c] Communion Office.

LECTURE XXIII.

Another Relation, to be brought under this Commandment, is, that between spiritual Fathers, the Teachers of Religion, and such as are to be taught.

The Duty of us who have undertaken the important Work of spiritual Guides and Teachers, is, to deliver the Doctrines and Precepts of our holy Religion, in the plainest and strongest Terms that we can; insisting on such Things chiefly, as will be most conducive to the real and inward Benefit of our Hearers; and recommending them, in the most prudent and persuasive Manner; *seeking to please all Men for their Good, to Edification*[d]; but fearing no Man in the Discharge of our Consciences; and neither saying nor omitting any Thing, for the Sake of Applause from the many, or the few: or of promoting either our own Wealth and Power, or that of our Order: to instruct, exhort, and comfort, all that are placed under our Care, with Sincerity, Discretion and Tenderness, privately as well as publickly, so far as they give us Opportunity, or we discern hope of doing Ser-

[d] Rom. xv. 2. 1 Cor. x. 33.

LECTURE XXIII.

vice; *watching for their Souls, as they that must give Account*[e]; to rule in the Church of God with Vigilance, Humility, and Meekness, *shewing ourselves, in all Things, Patterns of good Works*[f].

The Duty of you, the Christian Laity, whom we are to teach, is, to attend constantly and seriously on religious Worship and Instruction, as a sacred Ordinance appointed by Heaven for your spiritual Improvement; to consider impartially and carefully what you hear, and believe and practise what you are convinced you ought; to observe with due Regard the Rules established for decent Order and Edification in the Church; and pay such Respect, in Word and Deed, to those who minister to you in holy Things, as the Interest and Honour of Religion require; accepting and encouraging our well-meant Services, and bearing charitably with our many Imperfections and Failings.

A third Relation is that between Masters or Mistresses of Schools and their Scholars. The Duty of the former is, diligently to

[e] Heb. xiii. 17.   [f] Tit. ii. 7.

instruct

instruct the Children committed to them, in all the Things which they are put to learn, suiting their Manner of Teaching, as well as they can, to the Temper and Capacity of each; and to take effectual Care that they apply themselves to what is taught them, and do their best; to watch over their Behaviour, especially in the great Points of Honesty and Truth, Modesty and Good-Humour; shew Countenance to such as are well-behaved and promising; correct the Faulty, with needful, yet not with excessive Severity; and get the Incorrigible removed out of the Way, before they corrupt others. And the Duty of the Scholars is, to reverence and obey their Master or Mistress, as if they were their Parents; to live friendly and lovingly with one another, as Brethren or Sisters; to be heartily thankful to all, that give or procure them so valuable a Blessing as useful Knowledge; and industrious to improve in it; considering, how greatly their Happiness, here and hereafter, depends upon it.

LECTURE XXIII.

I come now to a fourth Relation, of great Extent and Importance, that between Heads of Families and their Servants.

When the New Teſtament was written, the Generality of Servants were, as in many Places they are ſtill, mere Slaves; and the Perſons to whom they belonged, had a Right to their Labour, and that of their Poſterity, for ever, without giving them any other Wages than their Maintenance; and with a Power to inflict on them what Puniſhments they pleaſed; for the moſt Part, even Death itſelf, if they would. God be thanked, Service amongſt us, is a much happier Thing; the Conditions of it being uſually no other, than the Servants themſelves voluntarily enter into, for their own Benefit. But then, for that Reaſon, they ought to perform whatever is due from them, both more conſcientiouſly, and more chearfully.

Now from Servants is due, in the firſt Place, Obedience. Indeed if they are commanded what is plainly unlawful, they *ought to obey God rather than Men*[g]; but ſtill muſt excuſe themſelves decently, though resolutely.

[f] Acts v. 29.

LECTURE XXIII.

resolutely. And even lawful Things, which they have not bargained to do, they are not obliged to do; nor any thing indeed, which is clearly and greatly unsuitable to their Place and Station, and improper to be required of them. But whatever they engaged, or knew they were expected, to do; or what, though they did not know of it beforehand, is usual and reasonable, or even not very unreasonable, they must submit to. For if they may, on every small Pretence, refuse to do *this*, and question whether *that* belongs to their Place, it is most evident, that all Authority and Order in Families must be at an End: and they themselves will have much more Trouble in disputing about their Business than they would have in performing it.

Servants therefore should obey; and they should do it respectfully and readily; not murmuring, behaving gloomily and sullenly, as if their Work were not due for their Wages; but, as the Apostle exhorts, *with Good-will doing Service*[h]; *not answering again*[i], and contradicting, as if those, whom they serve, were their Equals; but paying

[h] Eph. vi. 7.   [i] Tit. ii. 9.

all

LECTURE XXIII.

all fit Honour to their Master or Mistress, and to every one in the Family.

They are also to obey with Diligence: To spend as much Time in Work, and follow it as closely all that Time, as can be fairly expected from them; *not with Eye-Service, as Men-Pleasers,* (these are the Words of Scripture, twice repeated there) *but in Singleness of Heart, fearing God*[k]. Whatever Industry therefore a reasonable Master would require, when his eye is upon them, the same, in the main, honest Servants will use, when his Eye is not upon them: For his Presence or Absence can make no Difference in their Duty. He hath agreed with them for their Time and Pains; and he must not be defrauded of them.

With Diligence must always be joined Care, that no Business be neglected, or delayed beyond its proper Season; nothing mismanaged for want of thinking about it; nothing heedlessly, much less designedly, wasted and squandered; but all reasonable Frugality and good Contrivance shewn; and all fair Advantages taken, yet no other, for

[k] Eph. vi. 6. Col. iii. 22.

the Benefit of those who employ them. Every Servant would think this but common Justice in his own Case; and therefore should do it as common Justice in his Master's Case. Some perhaps may imagine, that their Master's Estate or Income is well able to afford them to be careless or extravagant. But the Truth is, few or no Incomes can afford this. For if it be practised in one Thing, why not in another? And what must follow, if it be practised in all? That certainly which we daily see, that Persons of the greatest Estates are distressed and ruined by it. Or though it would not distress them at all, yet a Master's Wealth is no more a Justification of Servants wasting what belongs to him, than of their stealing it: And if one be dishonest, the other must.

Now Dishonesty every body owns to be a Crime: but every body doth not consider sufficiently how many sorts of it there are. Observe then, that, besides the Instances already mentioned, and the gross ones that are punishable by Law, it is dishonest in a Servant, either to take to himself, or give to another, or consent to the taking or giving,

LECTURE XXIII.

ing, whatever he knows he is not allowed, and durst not do with his Master's Knowledge. There are, to be sure, various Degrees of this Fault; some not near so bad as others: but it is the same Kind of Fault in all of them: besides that the smaller Degrees lead to the greater. And all Dishonesty, bad as it is in other Persons, is yet worse in those who are intrusted as Servants are; and Things put in their Power upon that Trust; which if they break, they are unfaithful, as well as unjust.

Another Sort of Dishonesty is speaking Falsehoods: Against which I have already, in the Course of these Lectures, given some Cautions, and shall give more: therefore at present I shall only say, that, whether Servants are guilty of it amongst themselves, or to their Masters or Mistresses, whether against or in Favour of one another, or even in their own Favour, there are few Things, by which they may both do and suffer more Harm than a lying Tongue.

Truth therefore is a necessary Quality in Servants. And a further one is proper Secrecy. For there is great Unfairness in

betraying

betraying the Secrets, either of their Master's Business, or his Family; or turning to his Disadvantage any thing that comes to their Knowledge by being employed under him; unless it be where Conscience obliges them to a Discovery; which is a Case that seldom happens. And, excepting that Case, what they have promised to conceal, it is palpable Wickedness to disclose: And where they have not promised, yet they are taken into their Master's House to be Assistants and Friends, not Spies and Tale-Bearers; to do Service, not Harm, to him, and to every one that is under his Roof.

Two other Duties, of all Persons indeed, but in some Measure peculiarly of Servants, are—Sobriety, without which they can neither be careful nor diligent, nor will be likely to continue just; and Chastity, the Want of which will produce all Manner of Disorders and Mischiefs in the Family to which they belong, and utter Ruin to themselves.

The last requisite, which I shall mention, is Peaceableness and good Temper;

agreeable

LECTURE XXIII.

agreeing with and helping one another, and making the Work, which they have to do, eafy, and the Lives, which they are to lead together, comfortable. For it is very unfit, that either their Mafters or any other Part of the Family fhould fuffer through their Ill-humour: and indeed they fuffer enough by it themfelves, to make reftraining it well worth their while.

Thefe are the Duties of Servants: and as the faithful Performance of them is the fureft Way of ferving themfelves, and being happy in this World; fo, if it proceed from a true Principle of Confcience, God will accept it, as Service done to Himfelf, and make them eternally happy for it in the next: whereas wilfully tranfgreffing, or negligently flighting, the Things which they ought to do, whatever Pleafure, or whatever Advantage, it may promife or produce to them for a while, will feldom fail of bringing them at laft to Shame and Ruin even here, and will certainly bring them, unlefs they repent and amend, to Mifery hereafter.

But think not, I intreat you, that we will lay Burthens on thofe below us, and

Vol. II.   C   take

take none upon ourselves. There are Duties also, and very necessary ones, which Masters and Mistresses owe to their Servants.

To behave towards them with Meekness and Gentleness, not imperiously and with Contempt; and to restrain them, as far as may be, from giving bad Usage one to another; never to accuse, threaten, or suspect them, without or beyond Reason; to hear patiently their Defences and Complaints; and bear, with due Moderation, their Mistakes and Faults: neither to make them, when in Health, work or fare harder than is fitting; nor suffer them, when in Sickness, to want any Thing requisite for their Comfort and Relief: if they be hired Servants, to pay their Wages fully and punctually at the Time agreed: if they are put to learn any Business or Profession, to instruct them in it carefully and thoroughly; not only to give them Time for the Exercises of Religion; but Assistance to understand, and Encouragement to practise, every Part of their Duty: to keep them, as much as possible, both from Sin and Temptation, and particularly from corrupting each other:

to

LECTURE XXIII.

to shew Displeasure, when they do amiss, as far, and no farther than the Case requires; and to countenance and reward them, when they serve well, in Proportion to the Merit and Length of such Service. For all these Things are natural Dictates of Reason and Humanity; and clearly implied in that comprehensive Rule of Scripture: *Masters, give unto your Servants that which is just and equal; knowing that ye also have a Master in Heaven*[1].

There are still two Sorts more, of Inferiors and Superiors, that may properly be mentioned under this Commandment: young Persons and Elder; those of low and high Degree.

The Duty of the Younger is, to moderate their own Rashness and Love of Pleasure; to reverence the Persons and Advice of the Aged; and neither use them ill, nor despise them, on Account of the Infirmities that may accompany advanced Years; considering in what Manner they will expect hereafter that others should treat them. And the Duty of elder Persons is, to make

[1] Col. iv. 1.

all fit Allowances, but no hurtful ones, to the natural Difpofitions of young People: to inftruct them with Patience, and reprove them with Mildnefs; not to require either too much or too long Submiffion from them; but be willing that they, in their Turn, fhould come forward into the World; gradually withdrawing themfelves from the heavier Cares, and the lighter Pleafures, of this Life; and waiting with pious Refignation to be called into another.

The Duty of the lower Part of the World to thofe above them, in Rank, Fortune, or Office, is, not to envy them; or murmur at the Superiority, which a wife, though myfterious, Providence hath given them; but *in whatever State they are, therewith to be content* [m]; and pay willingly to others all the Refpect, which Decency or Cuftom have made their Due. At the fame Time, the Duty of thofe in higher Life is, to relieve the Poor, protect the Injured, countenance the Good, difcourage the Bad, as they have Opportunity; not to fcorn, much lefs to opprefs, the meaneft of their Brethren; but

[m] Phi'. iv. 11.

LECTURE XXIII.

to remember, that *we shall all stand before the Judgment-Seat of Christ*[n]; where *he that doth wrong, shall receive for the Wrong which he hath done; and there is no Respect of Persons*[o].

And now, were but all these Duties conscientiously observed by all the World, how happy a Place would it be! And whoever will faithfully do their own Part of them, they shall be happy, whether others will do theirs or not; and this Commandment assures them of it; *that thy Days may be long in the Land, which the Lord thy God giveth thee.* In all Probability, if we obey his Laws, and that now before us in particular, both longer and more prosperous will our Days prove in this Land of our Pilgrimage, in which God hath placed us to sojourn; but, without all Question, eternal and infinite shall our Felicity be, in that Land of Promise, the heavenly Canaan, which He hath appointed for our Inheritance; and which that we may all inherit accordingly, He of his Mercy grant, &c.

[n] Rom. xiv. 10   [o] Col. iii. 25.

LECTURE XXIV.

The Sixth Commandment.

HAVING set before you, under the Fifth Commandment, the particular Duties, which Inferiors and Superiors owe each to the other; I proceed now to those remaining Precepts, which express the general Duties of all Men to all Men.

Amongst these, as Life is the Foundation of every Thing valuable to us, the Preservation of it is justly intitled to the first Place. And accordingly the Sixth Commandment is, *Thou shalt do no Murder.* Murder is taking away a Person's Life, with Design, and without Authority. Unless both concur, it doth not deserve that Name.

1. It is not Murder, unless it be with Design. He, who is duly careful to avoid doing Harm, and unhappily, notwithstanding that, kills another, though he hath

Cause to be extremely forry for it, yet is entirely void of Guilt on Account of it. For his Will having no Share in the Action, it is not, in a moral Senfe, his. But if he do the Mifchief through Heedleffnefs, or Levity of Mind, or inconfiderate Vehemence, here is a Fault. If the Likelihood of Mifchief could be forefeen, the Fault is greater; and the higheft Degree of fuch Negligence, or impetuous Rafhnefs, comes near to bad Intention.

2. It is not Murder, unlefs it be without Authority. Now a Perfon hath Authority, from the Law both of God and Man, to defend his own Life, if he cannot do it otherwife, by the Death of whoever attacks it unjuftly: whofe Deftruction, in that Cafe, is of his own feeking, and *his Blood on his own Head*[a]. But nothing, fhort of the moft imminent Danger, ought ever to carry us to fuch an Extremity: and a good Perfon will fpare ever fo bad an one, as far as he can with any Profpect of Safety. Again, proper Magiftrates have Authority to fentence Offenders to Death, on fufficient Proof

[a] 2 Sam. i. 16. 1 Kings ii. 37. Ezek. xxxiii. 4.

LECTURE XXIV.

of such Crimes as the Welfare of the Community requires to be thus punished; and to employ others in the Execution of that Sentence. And private Persons have Authority, and in proper Circumstances are obliged, to seize and prosecute such Offenders: for all this is only another Sort of Self-Defence; defending the Public from what else would be pernicious to it. And the Scripture hath said, that the Sovereign Power *beareth not the Sword in vain*[b]. But in whatever Cases gentler Punishments would sufficiently answer the Ends of Government, surely capital ones are forbidden by this Commandment. Self-Defence, in the last Place, authorizes whole Nations to make war upon other Nations, when it is the only Way to obtain Redress of Injuries, which cannot be supported; or Security against impending Ruin. To determine, whether the State is indeed in these unhappy Circumstances, belongs to the supreme Jurisdiction: and the Question ought to be considered very conscientiously. For Wars begun or continued without

[b] Rom. xiii. 4.

Necessity,

Necessity, are unchristian and inhuman: as many Murders are committed, as Lives are lost in them; besides the innumerable Sins and Miseries of other Sorts, with which they are always attended. But Subjects, in their private Capacity, are incompetent Judges of what is requisite for the public Weal: nor can the Guardians of it permit them to act upon their Judgment, were they to make one. Therefore they may lawfully serve in Wars, which their Superiors have unlawfully undertaken, excepting perhaps such offensive Wars as are notoriously unjust. In others, it is no more the Business of the Soldiery to consider the Grounds of their Sovereign's taking up Arms, than it is the Business of the Executioner to examine whether the Magistrate hath passed a right Sentence.

You see then, in what Cases killing is not Murder: in all, but these, it is. And you cannot fail of seeing the Guilt of this Crime to be singularly great and heinous. It brings designedly upon one of our Brethren, without Cause, what human Nature abhors and dreads most. It cuts him off from all the

LECTURE XXIV.

Enjoyments of this Life at once, and sends him into another, for which possibly he was not yet prepared. It defaces the Image, and defeats the Design, of God. It overturns the great Purpose of Government and Laws, mutual Safety. It robs the Society of a Member, and consequently of Part of its Strength. It robs the Relations, Friends, and Dependants, of the Person destroyed, of every Benefit and Pleasure, which else they might have had from him. And the Injury done, in all these Respects, hath the terrible Aggravation, that it cannot be recalled. Most wisely therefore hath our Creator surrounded Murder with a peculiar Horror; that Nature, as well as Reason, may deter from it every one, who is not utterly abandoned to the worst of Wickedness: and most justly hath he appointed the Sons of *Noah*, that is, all Mankind, to punish Death with Death. *Whoso sheddeth Man's Blood, by Man shall his Blood be shed: for in the Image of God made He Man*[c]. And that nothing may protect so daring an Offender, he enjoined the *Jews*, in the Chapter which follows

[c] Gen. ix. 6.

lows the Ten Commandments; *If a Man come presumptuously upon his Neighbour to slay him with Guile, thou shalt take him from mine Altar, that he may die*[d]. But supposing, what seldom happens, that the Murderer may escape judicial Vengeance; yet what piercing Reflections, what continual Terrors and Alarms, must he carry about with him! And could he be hardened against these, it would only subject him the more inevitably to that future Condemnation, from which nothing but the deepest Repentance can possibly exempt him. For *no Murderer hath eternal Life*[e]; but they *shall have their Part in the Lake that burneth with Fire and Brimstone, which is the second Death*[f].

But shocking, and deserving of Punishment here and hereafter, as this Crime always is; yet there are Circumstances, which may augment it greatly. If the Person, whom any one deprives of Life, be placed in lawful Authority over him; or united in Relation or Friendship; to him or have done him Kindnesses; or only never have

[d] Exod. xxi. 14.   [e] 1 John iii. 15.   [f] Rev. xxi. 8.

done

LECTURE XXIV.

done him Harm; or be, in a peculiar Degree, good, useful, or pitiable; each of these Things considerably increases the Sin, though some indeed more than others. Again, if the horrid Fact be formally contrived, and perhaps the Design carried on through a Length of Time; this argues a much more steady and inflexible Depravity of Heart, than the Commission of it in a sudden Rage. But still, even the last, though it hath, in the Law of this Country, a different Name, of Man-Slaughter, given it, and a different Punishment prescribed for the first Offence; yet in the Sight of God is as truly Murder as the former, though freer from Aggravations. The Mischief done is done purposely; and neither Passion, nor Provocation, gives Authority for doing it, or even any great Excuse. For as God hath required us, he hath certainly enabled us, to restrain the hastiest Sallies of our Anger, especially from such Enormities as this.

Nor doth it materially alter the Nature, or lessen at all the Degree, of the Sin, if, whilst we attack another, we give him an

Opportunity to defend himself, and attack us: as in duelling. Still taking away his Life is Murder: expoſing our own is ſo likewiſe; as I ſhall quickly ſhew you. And an Appointment of two Perſons to meet for this Purpoſe, under Pretence of being bound to it by their Honour, is an Agreement in Form to commit, for the Sake of an abſurd Notion, or rather an unmeaning Word, the moſt capital Offence againſt each other, and their Maker; of which, if their Intention ſucceed, they cannot have Time to repent.

As to the Manner, in which Murder is committed; whether a Perſon do it directly himſelf, or employ another; whether he do it by Force, or Fraud, or Colour of Juſtice; accuſing falſely, or taking any unfair Advantage; theſe Things make little further Difference in the Guilt, than that the moſt artful and ſtudied Way is generally the worſt.

And though a Deſign of Murder ſhould not take Effect; yet whoever hath done all that he could towards it, is plainly as much a Sinner, as if it had. Nay, doing any Thing

LECTURE XXIV.

Thing towards it, or so much as once intending it, or assisting or encouraging any other who intends it, is the same Sort of Wickedness. And if a Person doth not directly design the Death of another; yet if he designedly doth what he knows or suspects may probably occasion it; he is, in Proportion to his Knowledge, or Suspicion, guilty. Nay, if he be only negligent in Matters, which may affect human Life; or meddles with them, when he hath Cause to think he understands them not; he is far from innocent. And there are several Professions and Employments, in which these Truths ought to be considered with a peculiar Degree of Seriousness.

Further yet: If it be criminal to contribute in any Manner towards taking away a Person's Life immediately; it must be criminal also to contribute any Thing towards shortening it, which is taking it away after a Time: whether by bringing any bodily Disease upon him, or causing him any Grief or Anxiety of Mind, or by what indeed will produce both, distressing him in his Circumstances: concerning which

which the Son of *Sirach* saith: *He that taketh away his Neighbour's Living, slayeth him; and he that defraudeth the Labourer of his Hire, is a Blood-Shedder* [g].

Indeed, if we cause or procure any Sort of Hurt to another, though it hath no Tendency to deprive him of Life, yet if it makes any Part of his Life, more or less, uneasy or uncomfortable, we deprive him so far of what makes it valuable to him: which is equivalent to taking so much of it away from him, or possibly worse.

Nay, if we do a Person no Harm; yet if we wish him Harm, St. *John* hath determined the Case: *Whosoever hateth his Brother is a Murderer* [h]. For indeed, Hatred not only leads to Murder; and too often, when indulged, produces it unexpectedly; but it is always, though perhaps for the most Part in a lower Degree, the very Spirit of Murder in the Heart; and it is by our Hearts that God will judge us. Nay, should our Dislike of another not rise to fixed Hatred and Malice; yet if it rise to unjust Anger, we know our Saviour's

[g] Ecclus. xxxiv. 92.   [h] 1 John. iii. 15.

Declaration.

LECTURE XXIV.

Declaration. *It was said by them of old Time, Thou shalt not kill: and whosoever shall kill, shall be in Danger of the Judgment. But I say unto you, whosoever is angry with his Brother without a Cause, shall be in Danger of the Judgment*[i]. That is, whosoever is angry, either with Persons that he ought not, or on Occasions that he ought not, or more vehemently, or sooner, or longer than he ought, is guilty in some Measure of that uncharitableness of which Murder is the highest Act; and liable to the Punishment of it in the same Proportion.

Nor even yet have I carried the Explanation of this Commandment to the Extent of our Duty. Whoever doth not, as far as can be reasonably expected from him, endeavour to guard his Neighbour from Harm, to make Peace, to relieve Distress and Want, fails of what Love to human Kind certainly requires. Now *Love is the fulfilling of the Law*[k]: and *he that loveth not his Brother, abideth in Death*[l].

We are also carefully to observe, that however heinous it is, to sin against the

---
[i] Matt. v. 21, 22. [k] Rom. xiii. 10. [l] 1 John iii. 14.

temporal

temporal Life of any one: injuring him in respect of his eternal Interests, is yet unspeakably worse. If it be unlawful to kill or hurt the Body, or overlook Men's worldly Necessities; much more is it to *destroy* the Soul of *our Brother, for whom Christ died*[m]; or any Way endanger it; or even suffer it to continue in Danger, if we have in our Power the proper and likely Means of delivering it. And on the other Hand, all that Mercy and Humanity, which, in the civil Concerns of our Neighbours, is so excellent a Duty, must proportionably be still more excellent in their religious ones, and of higher Value in the Sight of God.

Hitherto I have considered the Prohibition, *Thou shalt do no Murder*, as respecting others: but it forbids also Self-Murder. As we are not to commit Violence against the Image of God in the Person of any of our Brethren; so neither in our own. As we are not to rob the Society to which we belong, or any Part of it, of the Service, which any other of its Members might do it; we are not to rob either of what we

[m] Rom. xiv. 15.

might

LECTURE XXIV.

might do. As we are not to send any one else out of the World prematurely; we are not to send ourselves; but *wait* with Patience *all the Days of our appointed Time, till our Change come*[n]. If the Sins, which Persons have committed, prompt them to Despair; they of all others, instead of rushing into the Presence of God by adding this dreadful one to them, should earnestly desire *Space to repent*[o]; which, by his Grace, the worst of Sinners may do, and be forgiven. If their Misfortunes or Sufferings make them weary of Life; he hath sent them these with Design, that they should not by unlawful Means evade them, but go through them well: whether they be inflicted for the Punishment of their Faults, or the Trial of their Virtues. In either Case, we are to submit quietly to the Discipline of our heavenly Father: which he will not suffer to be heavier than we can bear, whatever we may imagine; but will support us under it, improve us by it, and in due Time release us from it. But in any Case for Persons to make away with them-

[n] Job. xiv. 14.   [o] Rev. ii. 21.

selves, is to arraign the Conſtitution of Things which he hath appointed; and to refuſe living where he hath put them to live: a very provoking Inſtance of Undutifulneſs, and made peculiarly fatal by this Circumſtance, that leaving uſually no Room for Repentance, it leaves none for Pardon: always excepting, where it proceeds from a Mind ſo diſordered by a bodily Diſeaſe, as to be incapable of judging or acting reaſonably. For God knows with Certainty when this is the Cauſe, and when not: and will accordingly either make due Allowances, or make none.

And if deſtroying ourſelves be a Sin, doing any Thing wilfully or heedleſsly, that tends to our Deſtruction, muſt in Proportion be a Sin. Where indeed Neceſſity requires great Hazards to be run by ſome Perſons for the Good of others: as in War, in extinguiſhing dangerous Fires, in ſeveral Caſes which might be named; or where Employments and Profeſſions which ſomebody or other muſt undertake, or ſuch Diligence in any Employment as Men are by Accidents really called to uſe, impair Health

and

and shorten Life; there, far from being thrown away, it is laudably spent in the Service of God and Man. But for any Person to bring on himself an untimely End, by adventurous Rashness, by ungoverned Passion, by immoderate Anxiety, or by an obstinate or careless Neglect of his own Preservation, is unquestionably sinful. And above all, doing it by Debauchery or immoral Excess, is a most effectual Way of ruining Soul and Body at once.

Let us therefore be conscientiously watchful against every Thing which may provoke, or entice us, to be injurious, either to others or ourselves. And God grant, that we may so regard the Lives of our Fellow-Creatures, and so employ our own, that we may ever please the Giver and Lord of Life: and having faithfully lived to him here, may eternally live with him hereafter, through Jesus Christ our only Saviour. Amen.

LECTURE XXV.

The Seventh Commandment.

IN speaking to this Commandment, it is proper to begin with observing, that as in the Sixth, where Murder is forbidden, every Thing which tends to it, or proceeds from the same bad Principle with it, is forbidden too: so here, in the Seventh, where Adultery is prohibited, the Prohibition must be extended to whatever else is criminal in the same Kind. And therefore in explaining it, I shall treat, first of the Fidelity which it requires from married Persons, and then of the Chastity and Modesty which it requires from all Persons.

First of the Fidelity owing to each other from married Persons.

Not only the Scripture-Account of the Creation of Mankind is a Proof to as many as believe in Scripture, that the Union of one Man with one Woman was the original Design and Will of Heaven; but the remarkable Equality of Males and Females born into the World is an Evidence of it to all Men. Yet notwithstanding, it must be owned, the Cohabitation of one Man with several Wives at the same Time was practised very anciently in the darker Ages, even by some of the Patriarchs, who were otherwise good Persons; but, having no explicit revealed Rule concerning this Matter, failed of discerning the above-mentioned Purpose of God. And both this Error and that of Divorce on slight Occasions, were tolerated by the Law of *Moses*. But that was only as the Laws of other Countries often connive at what the Lawgiver is far from approving. Accordingly God expressed, particularly by the Prophet *Malachi*[a], his Dislike of these Things. And our Saviour both tells the Jews, that *Moses* permitted Divorces at Pleasure, merely *because of the Hardness of their Hearts*, and peremptorily declares, that *whosoever shall put away his Wife, except it be for Forni-*

[a] Mal. ii. 14, 15, 16.

cation,

LECTURE XXV.

cation, and shall marry another, committeth Adultery[b]. Now certainly it cannot be less adulterous to marry a Second without putting away the First.

Nor is Polygamy (that is, the having more Wives than one at once) prohibited in holy Writ alone, but condemned by many of the Heathens themselves, who alledge against it very plain and forcible Reasons. It is inconsistent with a due Degree of mutual Affection in the Parties, and due Care in the Education of their Children. It introduces into Families perpetual Subjects of the bitterest Enmity and Jealousy; keeps a Multitude of Females in most unnatural Bondage, frequently under Guardians fitted for the Office by unnatural Cruelty; and tempts a Multitude of Males, thus left unprovided for, to unnatural Lusts. In civilized and well-regulated Countries therefore, single Marriages have either been established at first, or prevailed afterwards on Experience of their Preferableness: and a mutual Promise of inviolable Faithfulness to the Marriage-Bed hath been understood

Matth. xix. 8, 9.

LECTURE XXV.

to be an essential Part of the Contract: which Promise is with us most solemnly expressed in the Office of Matrimony, by as clear and comprehensive Words as can be devised. And unless Persons are at Liberty in all Cases to slight the most awful Vows to God, and the most deliberate Engagements of each to the other; how can they be at Liberty in this, where public Good and private Happiness are so deeply interested?

Breaches of plighted Faith, as they must be preceded by a Want of sufficient conjugal Affection in the offending Party, so they tend to extinguish all the Remains of it: and this Change will be perceived, and will give Uneasiness to the Innocent one, though the Cause be hid. But if it be known, or merely suspected by the Person wronged, (which it seldom fails to be in a little Time) it produces from the Make of the human Mind, in warmer Tempers, a Resentment so strong, in milder, an Affliction so heavy, that few Things in the World equal either. *For Love is strong as Death, Jealousy is cruel as the Grave, the Coals*

LECTURE XXV.

Coals thereof are Coals of Fire[c]. And, with whatever Vehemence they burn inwardly or outwardly, it can be no Wonder; when perfidious Unkindness is found in that nearest Relation, where Truth and Love were deliberately pledged, and studiously paid on one Side in Expectation of a suitable Return; and when the tenderest Part of the Enjoyment of Life is given up beyond Recall into the Hands of a Traitor, who turns it into the acutest Misery. To what a Height Grief and Anger on one Side, and Neglect ripened into Scorn and Hatred on the other, may carry such Calamities, cannot be foreseen: but at least they utterly destroy that Union of Hearts, that reciprocal Confidence, that Openness of Communication, that Sameness of Interests, of Joys and of Sorrows, which constitute the principal Felicity of the married State. And besides, how very frequently do the Consequences of these Transgressions affect, and even ruin, the Health or the Fortune, it may be both, of the blameless Person in common with the other: and

[c] Cant. viii. 6.

perhaps

perhaps derive down Diseases and Poverty to successive Generations!

These are Fruits which Unfaithfulness in either Party may produce. In one it may produce yet more. A Woman, guilty of this Crime, who, to use the Words of Scripture, *forsaketh the Guide of her Youth, and forgetteth the Covenant of her God*[d], brings peculiar Disgrace on her Husband, her Children, and Friends; and may bring an illegitimate Offspring to inherit what is the Right of others; nor is the Infamy and Punishment, to which she exposes herself, a less dreadful Evil for being a deserved one. And if Falsehood on the Men's Part hath not all the same Aggravations, it hath very great ones in their Stead. They are almost constantly the Tempters: they often carry on their wicked Designs for a long Time together: they too commonly use the vilest Means to accomplish them. And as they claim the strictest Fidelity, it is ungenerous, as well as unjust, to fail of paying it. All Men must feel how bitter it would be to them to be injured in this Respect; let them

[d] Prov. ii. 17.

think

LECTURE XXV.

think then what it is to be injurious in it: and since the Crime is the same when committed by them, as when committed against them, let them own that it deserves the same Condemnation from the Judge of the World. *The Lord hath been Witness*, saith the Prophet, *between thee and the Wife of thy Youth, against whom thou dealest treacherously; yet is she thy Companion, and the Wife of thy Covenant. Therefore take Heed to your Spirit, and let none deal treacherously with the Wife of his Youth* [e].

It will be safest, but I hope it is not necessary, to add, that an unmarried Man or Woman, offending with the Wife or Husband of any one, being no less guilty of Adultery than the Person with whom the Offence is committed, is consequently an Accomplice in all the Wickedness and all the Mischief abovementioned; and this frequently with aggravating Circumstances of the greatest Baseness, and Treachery, and Ingratitude, and Cruelty, that can be imagined. Whatever some may plead, surely none can think such Behaviour defensible;

[e] Mal. ii. 14, 15.

and

and most surely they will not find it so: for *Marriage is honourable in all, and the Bed undefiled; but Whoremongers and Adulterers God will judge* [f].

The Crime of Adultery being so great, it follows, that all improper Familiarities, which, though undesignedly, may lead to Adultery, and all imprudent Behaviour, which may give Suspicion of it, is to be avoided as Matter of Conscience; that all groundless Jealousy is to be checked by those who are inclined to it, and discouraged by others, as most heinous Injustice; and that every Thing should be carefully observed by both Parties, which may endear them to each other. No Persons therefore should ever enter into the Marriage-Bond with such as they cannot esteem and love: and all Persons, who have entered into it, should use all Means, not only to preserve Esteem and Love, but to increase it: affectionate Condescension on the Husband's Part, cheerful Submission on the Wife's; Mildness and Tenderness, Prudence and Attention to their common Interest,

[f] Heb. xiii. 4.

LECTURE XXV.

and that of their joint Posterity, on both Parts. It is usually, in a great Measure at least, from the Want of these engaging Qualities in one or the other, that Falsehood arises. And if that doth not, some other Evil will; too likely to produce Effects equally grievous, and therefore to be considered as equally forbidden.

But now, from the mutual Fidelity required of married Persons, I proceed, secondly, to the Chastity and Modesty required of all Persons.

Supposing that only such as live single were to be guilty with each other; yet by Means even of this Licentiousness, in Proportion as it prevails, the Regularity and good Order of Society is overturned, the Credit and Peace of Families destroyed, the proper Disposal of young People in Marriage prevented, the due Education of Children and Provision for them neglected, the keenest Animosities perpetually excited, and the most shocking Murders frequently committed, of the Parties themselves, their Rivals, their innocent Babes: in short, every Enormity follows from hence, that lawless Passion

Paſſion can introduce. For all Sins indeed, but eſpecially this, leads Perſons on to more and greater: to all Manner of Falſehood to ſecure their Succeſs, all Manner of Diſhoneſty to provide for the Expenſiveneſs of theſe Courſes, all Manner of Barbarity to hide the Shame or lighten the Inconveniences of them: till thus they become abandoned to every Crime, by indulging this one.

But let us conſider the fatal Effects of it on the two Sexes, ſeparately. Women, that loſe their Innocence, which ſeldom fails of being ſoon diſcovered, loſe their good Name entirely along with it; are marked out and given up at once to almoſt irrecoverable Infamy: and even mere Suſpicion hath in ſome Meaſure the ſame bad Conſequences with certain Proof. It is, doubtleſs, extremely unjuſt to work up mere Imprudences into groſs Tranſgreſſions: and even the greateſt Tranſgreſſors ought to be treated with all poſſible Compaſſion, when they appear truly penitent. But, unleſs they appear ſo, a wide Diſtinction between them and others ought to be made. And they who

LECTURE XXV.

who contribute, whether defignedly or thoughtlefsly, to place good, bad, and doubtful Characters all on a Level, do moft prepofteroufly obfcure and debafe their own Virtue, if they have any; keep Guilt in Countenance, and defraud right Conduct of the peculiar Efteem which belongs to it: thus injuring at once the Caufe of Religion and Morals, and the Interefts of Society. But befides the general Difregard, of which vicious Women will experience not a little, even in Places and Times of the moft relaxed Ways of thinking, they have a forer Evil to expect; of being, fooner or later, for the moft part very foon, caft off and abandoned, with Contempt and Scorn, by their Seducers. Or even fhould they have Reparation made them by Marriage; this doth not take away the Sin at all, and the Difgrace but very imperfectly: not to fay, that it ftill leaves them peculiarly expofed to the Reproaches and the Jealoufy of their Hufbands ever after.

And if Men, that feduce Women, are not looked on by the World with fo much Abhorrence, as Women that are feduced, at least they deserve to be looked on with greater. For there cannot easily be more exquisite Wickedness, than, merely for the gratifying of a brutal Appetite or idle Fancy, to change all the Prospect, which a young Person hath of being happy and respected through Life, into Guilt, and Dishonour, and Distress, out of which too probably she will never be disentangled, under the false and treacherous Pretence of tender Regard. If we have any Feeling of Conscience within us, we must feel this to be most unworthy Behaviour. And if the Ruler of the World hath any Attention to the moral Character of his rational Creatures, which is the noblest Object of his Attention, that can be conceived, He must shew it on such Occasions: and therefore may be believed, when He saith He will.

But supposing Men not to corrupt the Innocent, but to sin with such alone as make a Profession of Sin; yet even this Manner of breaking the Law of God hath most dreaful Consequences. It hinders the Increase of a Nation in general. It leaves the few Children, that proceed from these Mixtures,

LECTURE XXV.

tures, abandoned to Misery, Uselessness and Wickedness. It turns aside the Minds of Persons from beneficial and laudable Employments to mean sensual Pursuits. It encourages and increases the most dissolute and in every Sense abandoned Set of Wretches in the World, common Prostitutes, to their own miserable and early Destruction; and that of Multitudes of unwary Youths, who would else have escaped. It debases the Heart, by the Influence of such vile and profligate Company, to vile and profligate Ways of thinking and acting. It sometimes produces Quarrels, that are immediately fatal: sometimes Friendships, that are equally so, to every valuable Purpose of Life. It leads Men to Extravagance and Profusion, grieves all that wish them well, distresses those who are to support them, and drives them to the most criminal Methods of supporting themselves. It tempts Men to Excesses and Irregularities of every Kind, wastes their Health and Strength, brings on them painful and opprobrious Diseases, too often communicated to those, whom they afterwards marry; and to their miserable Posterity, if they

they have any. By all these Mischiefs, which for the most Part come upon them in the Beginning of their Days, the Remainder of them is usually made either *short* or *tedious*, perhaps both [g]. With great Wisdom therefore doth Solomon exhort: *Remove thy Way from the strange Woman, and come not nigh the Door of her House: lest thou give thine Honour unto others, and thy Years unto the Cruel: lest Strangers be filled with thy Wealth, and thou mourn at the last, when thy Flesh and thy Body are consumed, and say, How have I hated Instruction, and my Heart despised Reproof; and I have not obeyed the Voice of my Teachers. For the Ways of Man are before the Eyes of the Lord, and he pondereth all his Goings. His own Iniquities shall take the Wicked, and he shall be holden with the Cords of his Sins* [h].

It is very true, the Sins of the Flesh do not always produce all the bitter Fruits which I have mentioned. But then such Instances of them, as at first are imagined the safest, frequently prove extremely hurtful; or however entice Persons on to worse,

[g] Wisd. ii. 1.   [h] Prov. v. 8 -13, 21, 22.

till

LECTURE XXV.

till they come at length to the moſt flagrant and pernicious. Very few, who tranſgreſs the Scripture-Bounds, ever ſtop at thoſe Lengths, which themſelves, when they ſet out, thought the greateſt that were defenſible. Liberties taken by Men before Marriage, incline them to repeat the ſame Liberties after Marriage; and alſo to entertain the moſt injurious Jealouſies of good Women, grounded on the Knowledge which they have formerly had of bad ones. Their paſt Succeſſes embolden and encite them to new and more flagitious Attempts: and by Appetites thus indulged, and Habits contracted, they are carried on perpetually further and further, till they come to be guilty, and ſometimes merely for the Sake and the Name of being guilty, of what they would once have trembled to hear propoſed.

But ſuppoſing they keep within the Limits of what they at firſt imagined to be allowable: is Imagination (and Reaſon, when biaſſed by Paſſions, is nothing better) the Teſt of Truth? Suppoſing their Behaviour could be harmleſs otherwiſe, is not the Example dangerous? Will or can the World around

around them take Notice of all the pretended Peculiarities that diftinguifh their Cafe, and preferve it from being a Sin, while other Crimes, to which at firft Sight it is very like, are confeffedly great ones? or will not all, who have bad Inclinations or unfettled Principles, take Shelter under their Practice, and either defpife their Refinements, or eafily invent fimilar ones for their own Ufe?

But further yet: if it be argued, that Offences of this Nature may by Circumftances be rendered excufable, why not others alfo? why may not Robbery, why may not Murder, be defended, by faying, that though undoubtedly in general they are very wrong, yet in fuch or fuch particular Occurrences, there is on the whole very little Hurt, or none at all, done by them, but perhaps Good? And what would become of the human Race, were fuch Pleas admitted? The Ends of Government can be attained by no other than by plain, determinate, comprehenfive Laws, to be fteadily obferved: and no one's Inclination, or fanciful Theories, are to decide,

LECTURE XXV.

cide, when they bind, and when not: but Deviations from them are criminal, if on no other Account, yet becaufe they are Deviations: though differently criminal indeed according to their different Degrees. Thus in the Matter before us, what approaches nearer to Marriage is, ordinarily fpeaking, fo far lefs blameable, than what is more diftant from it: but nothing can be void of Blame, and of great Blame, that breaks the Ordinances of God or Man. For even the latter, if they oblige the Confcience in any Cafe, muft oblige it in this, where public and private Welfare is fo effentially concerned. And as to the former, though fenfual Irregularities may fuit very well with fome Sorts of Superftition, yet their Inconfiftence with any Thing that deferves the Name of Religion, is confeffed in Effect by the Perfons guilty of them. For if fome few fuch do hypocritically, in vain Hope of Concealment, keep on the Appearance of it, yet who amongft them can preferve the Reality of it? Offences of this Kind, how plaufible foever palliated, yet, being committed againft known Prohibitions,

tions, wear out of the Mind all Reverence to God's Commandments, all Expectation of his future Favour, nay the very Defire of fpiritual Happinefs hereafter. And though many, who indulge in Licentioufnefs, have notwithftanding very good Qualities; yet, would they review their Hearts and Lives, they would find that they have much the fewer for it; and that thofe which remain are often made ufelefs, often endangered, often perverted by it.

But the Sins already mentioned, are by no means the only ones to be avoided in Confequence of this Commandment: whatever invites to them, whatever approaches towards them, whatever is contrary to Decency and Honour, whatever taints the Purity of the Mind, inflames the Paffions, and wears off the Impreffions of virtuous Shame; all Immodefty of Appearance or Behaviour; all Entertainments, Books, Pictures, Converfations, tending to excite or excufe the Indulgence of irregular Defires, are in their Proportion prohibited and criminal. And unlefs we prudently guard againft the fmaller Offences of this Kind,

the

LECTURE XXV.

the more heinous will be too likely to force their Way: as our Lord very strongly warns us. *Ye have heard, it was said by them of old Time, Thou shalt not commit Adultery: but I say unto you, that whosoever looketh on a Woman to lust after her, hath committed Adultery with her already in his Heart*[j]. And though vicious Inclinations were never to go further than the Heart; yet if, instead of merely intruding against our Will, they are designedly encouraged to dwell there, they corrupt the very Fountain of spiritual Life; and none but *the pure in Heart shall see God*[k].

All Persons therefore should be very careful to turn their Minds from forbidden Objects, to fix their Attention so constantly and steadily on useful and commendable Employments, as to have no Leisure for Vices, and to govern themselves by such Rules of Temperance and Prudence, that every sensual Appetite may be kept in Subjection to the Dictates of Reason and the Laws of Religion; always remembering that Christianity both delivers to us the strictest

[j] Matth. v. 27, 28.   [k] Matth. v. 8.

Precepts

Precepts of Holiness, and sets before us the strongest Motives to it; our peculiar Relation to a holy God and Saviour; our being *the Temples of the Holy Ghost*[l], which *Temple if any Man defile, him will God destroy*[m]; our being *Pilgrims and Strangers on Earth*[n], not intended to have our Portion here, but to inherit a spiritual Happiness hereafter: and *every one that hath this Hope, must purify himself even as God is pure*[o]. I shall conclude therefore with St. *Paul*'s Exhortation: *Fornication and all Uncleanness, let it not be once named among you, as becometh Saints; neither Filthiness, nor foolish Talking, nor Jesting, which are not convenient: for this ye know, that no Whoremonger, nor unclean Person, hath any Inheritance in the Kingdom of Christ and of God. Let no Man deceive you with vain Words: for because of these Things cometh the Wrath of God upon the Children of Disobedience. Be not ye therefore Partakers with them: walk as Children of Light, and have no Fellowship with the unfruitful Works of Darkness*[p].

[l] 1 Cor. vi. 19.   [m] 1 Cor. iii. 17.   [n] 1 Pet. ii. 11.
[o] 1 John iii. 3.   [p] Eph. v. 3—11.

LECTURE XXVI.

The Eighth Commandment.

UNDER the Eighth Commandment is comprehended our Duty to our Neighbour, in refpect of his worldly Subftance. And, to explain it diftinctly, I fhall endeavour to fhew,

I. What it forbids: and
II. What, by Confequence, it requires.

I. As to the former. The Wickednefs of Mankind hath invented Ways to commit fuch an aftonifhing Variety of Sins againft this Commandment, that it is impoffible to reckon them up, and dreadful to think of them. But moft, if not all of them, are fo manifeftly Sins, that the leaft Reflection is enough to make any one fenfible, how much he is bound confcientioufly to avoid them. And he, who defires to preferve himfelf innocent, eafily may.

LECTURE XXVI.

The moſt open and ſhameleſs Crime, of this Sort, is Robbery; taking from another what is his, by Force: which, adding Violence againſt his Perſon to Invaſion of his Property, and making every Part of human Life unſafe, is a complicated Tranſgreſſion, of very deep Guilt.

The next Degree is ſecret Theft: privately converting to our own Uſe what is not our own. To do this in Matters of great Value, is confeſſedly pernicious Wickedneſs. And though it were only in what may ſeem a Trifle; yet every Man's Right to the ſmalleſt Part of what belongs to him is the ſame, as to the largeſt, and he ought no more to be wronged of one, than of the other. Beſides, little Inſtances of Diſhoneſty cauſe great Diſquiet: make the Sufferers diſtruſtful of all about them; ſometimes of thoſe, who are the fartheſt from deſerving it: make them apprehenſive continually, that ſome heavier Injury will follow. And indeed almoſt all Offenders begin with ſlight Offences. More heinous ones would ſhock them at firſt; but if they once allow themſelves in leſſer Faults; they go

on

LECTURE XXVI.

on without Reluctance, by Degrees, to worse and worse, till at last they scruple nothing. Always therefore beware of small Sins. And always remember what I have already observed to you, that when any Thing is committed to your Care and Trust, to be dishonest in that, is peculiarly base.

But, besides what every body calls Theft, there are many Practices, which amount indirectly to much the same Thing, however disguised in the World under gentler Names. Thus, in the Way of Trade, and Business: if the Seller puts off any Thing for better than it is, by false Assertions, or deceitful Arts: if he takes Advantage of the Buyer's Ignorance, or particular Necessities, or good Opinion of him, to insist on a larger Price for it, than the current Value; or if he gives less in Quantity than he professes, or is understood to give: the Frequency of some of these Things cannot alter the Nature of any of them: no one can be ignorant that they are wrong, but such as are wilfully or very carelessly ignorant: and the Declaration of Scripture against the last of them is extended, in the same Place, to every one of the

Rest.

Rest. *Thou shalt not have in thy Bag divers Weights, a great and a small: thou shalt not have in thine House divers Measures, a great and a small. For all that do such Things, and all that do unrighteously, are an Abomination unto the Lord thy God* [a].

On the other Hand: if the Buyer takes Advantage of his own Wealth; and the Poverty or present Distress of the Seller, to beat down the Price of his Merchandise beyond Reason; or if he buys up the whole of a Commodity, especially if it be a necessary one, to make immoderate Gain of it; or if he refuses or neglects to pay for what he hath bought; or delays his Payments beyond the Time, within which, by Agreement or the known Course of Traffic, they ought to be made: all such Behaviour is downright Injustice and Breach of God's Law. For the Rule is, *If thou sellest ought unto thy Neighbour, or buyest ought of thy Neighbour's Hand, ye shall not oppress one another* [b].

---

[a] Deut. xxv. 13—16.   [b] Lev. xxv. 14.

Again:

LECTURE XXVI.

Again: Borrowing on fraudulent Securities, or false Representations of our Circumstances, or without Intention, or without proper Care afterwards, to repay; preferring the Gratification of our Covetousness, our Vanity, our Voluptuousness, our Indolence, before the satisfying of our just Debts: all this is palpable Wickedness. And just as bad is the contrary Wickedness, of demanding exorbitant Interest for lending to ignorant or thoughtless Persons; or to extravagant ones, for carrying on their Extravagance; or to necessitous ones, whose Necessities it must continually increase, and make their Ruin, after a while, more certain, more difficult to retrieve, and more hurtful to all with whom they are concerned. The Scripture hath particularly forbidden it in the last Case, and enjoined a very different Sort of Behaviour. *If thy Brother be waxen poor, and fallen in Decay with thee; then shalt thou relieve him: yea, though he be a Stranger, or a Sojourner. Thou shalt not give him thy Money upon Usury, nor lend him thy Victuals for Increase; but fear thy God, that thy Brother may dwell with*

LECTURE XXVI.

with thee [c]. And the Psalmist hath expressed the two opposite Characters, on these Occasions, very briefly and clearly. *The wicked borroweth, and payeth not again: but the Righteous sheweth Mercy, and giveth* [d].

Another crying Iniquity is, when hired Servants, Labourers, or Workmen of any Sort, are ill used in their Wages: whether by giving them too little; or, which is often full as bad, deferring it too long: The Word of God forbids this last in very strong Terms. *Thou shalt not defraud thy Neighbour, neither rob him: the Wages of him that is hired, shall not abide with thee,* meaning, if demanded or wanted, *all Night until the Morning* [e]. *At his Day shalt thou give him his Hire; neither shall the Sun go down upon it; for* [f] *he is poor; and setteth his Heart upon it: lest he cry against thee unto the Lord, and it be Sin unto thee* [g]. Nay, the Son of *Sirach* carries it, with Reason, (as I observed to you on the Sixth Commandment) further still. *The Bread of the*

---

[c] Lev. xxv. 35, &c.   [d] Psalm. xxxvii. 21.   [e] Lev. xix. 13.
[f] For—or, *when*.   [g] Deut. xxiv. 15.

Needy

LECTURE XXVI.

Needy is their Life: he that defraudeth the Labourer of his Hire, is a Blood-Shedder [h].

But, besides all these Instances of Unrighteousness, there are many more that are frequent in all Kinds of Contracts. Driving Bargains, that we know are too hard; or insisting rigidly on the Performance of them, after they appear to be so: making no Abatements, when bad Times, or unexpected Losses, or other Alterations of Circumstances, call for them: not inquiring into the Grounds of Complaints, when there is a Likelihood of their being just: throwing unreasonable Burthens upon others, merely because they dare not refuse them: keeping them to the very Words and Letter of an Agreement, contrary to the equitable Intention of it; or, on the other Hand, alledging some Flaw and Defect in Form, to get loose from an Agreement, which ought to have been strictly observed: all these Things are grievous Oppressions. And though some of them may not be in the least contrary to Law, yet they are utterly irreconcileable with good Conscience. Hu-

[h] Ecclus. xxxiv. 21, 22.

man Laws cannot provide for all Cases: and sometimes the vilest Iniquities may be committed under their Authority, and by their Means.

It is therefore a further lamentable Breach of this Commandment, when one Person puts another to the Charge and Hazard of Law unjustly or needlesly; or, in ever so necessary a Law-Suit, occasions unnecessary Expences, and contrives unfair Delays: in short when any thing is done by either Party; by the Counsel, that plead or advise in the Cause, or by the Judge, who determines it, contrary to real Justice and Equity.

Indeed when Persons, by any Means whatever, withhold from another his Right; either keeping him ignorant of it, or forcing him to unreasonable Cost or Trouble to obtain it; this, in its Proportion, is the same Kind of Injury with stealing from him. To see the Rich and Great, in these or any Ways, bear hard upon the Poor, is very dreadful: and truly it is little, if at all, less so, when the lower Sort of People are unmerciful, as they are but too often, one to another. For, s *Solomon* observes,

A poor

LECTURE XXVI.

A poor Man that oppresseth the Poor, is like a sweeping Rain, which leaveth no Food[i]. But suppose it to be a Person ever so wealthy, that is wronged; still his Wealth is his own, and no one can have more Right to take the least Part of it from him, without his Consent, than to rob the meanest Wretch in the World. Suppose it be a Body or Number of Men; suppose it to be the Government, the Public, that is cheated; be it of more or less, be it of so little as not to be sensibly missed; let the Guilt be divided amongst ever so many; let the Practice be ever so common; still it is the same Crime, however it may vary in Degrees: and the Rule is without Exception, that *no Man go beyond, or defraud his Brother in any Matter*[k].

It surely scarce needs to be added, that whatever Things it is unlawful to do, it is also unlawful to advise, encourage, help, or protect others in doing: that buying, receiving, or concealing stolen Goods, knowing them to be such, is becoming a Partner in the Stealth: and that

[i] Prov. xxviii. 3.   [k] 1 Thess. iv. 6.

being any Way a Patron, Affiftant, or Tool of Injuftice, is no lefs evidently wrong, than being the immediate and principal Agent in it.

And as the Wrongnefs of all thefe Things is very plain, fo is the Folly of them. Common Robbers and Thieves are the moft miferable Set of Wretches upon Earth: in perpetual Danger, perpetual Frights and Alarms; obliged to fupport their Spirits by continual Exceffes, which, after the gay Madnefs of a few Hours, deprefs them to the moft painful Lownefs; confined to the moft hateful and hellifh Society; very foon, generally fpeaking, betrayed by their deareft Companions, or hunted out by vigilant Officers; then fhut up in Horror, condemned to open Shame, if not to an untimely Death; and the more furely undone for ever in the next Life, the more infenfible they are of their Sufferings and their Sins in this.

Nor do they, of whofe Guilt the Law can take little or no Cognizance, efcape a heavy and bitter Self-Condemnation from Time to Time; nor ufually the bad Opinion of

LECTURE XXVI.

of the World; which laſt alone will frequently do them more Harm, than any unfair Practices will do them Good. But eſpecially this holds in the middle and lower, which is vaſtly the larger, Part of Mankind. Their Livelihood depends chiefly on their Character; and their Character depends on their Honeſty. This will make Amends for many other Defects; but nothing will make Amends for the Want of this. Deceitful Craft may ſeem perhaps a ſhorter Method of Gain, than Uprightneſs and Diligence. But they, who get wickedly, ſpend, for the moſt Part, fooliſhly, perhaps wickedly too: and ſo that all that ſtays by them is their Guilt. Or let them be ever ſo cunning, and appear for a while to thrive ever ſo faſt; yet remember the Sayings of the wiſe King: *An Inheritance may be gotten haſtily at the Beginning; but the End thereof ſhall not be bleſſed*[l]. *Treaſures of Wickedneſs profit nothing: but Righteouſneſs delivereth from Death*[m]. *Wealth, gotten by Vanity, ſhall be diminiſhed: but he that gathereth by Labour, ſhall increaſe*[n]. Or, ſhould the Proſperity of Perſons, who raiſe

[l] Prov. xx. 21. [m] Prov. x. 2. [n] Prov. xiii. 11.

themſelves

LECTURE XXVI.

themselves by ill Means, last as long as their Lives; yet their Lives may be cut short. For what the Prophet threatens, often comes to pass, and is always to be feared: *He that getteth Riches, and not by Right, shall leave them in the Midst of his Days, and at his End shall be a Fool*[o]. But should his Days on Earth be extended to the utmost; yet *the Sinner, an hundred Years old shall be accursed*[p]. For *the Unrighteous shall not inherit the Kingdom of God*[q]: but *the Lord is the Avenger of all such*[r].

Let every one therefore consider seriously, in the first Place, what this Commandment forbids; and abstain from it. Though he fare more hardly; though he lay up less; though he be despised for his Conscientiousness, provided it be a reasonable one; surely it is well worth while to bear these Things, rather than injure our Fellow-Creatures, and offend our Maker.

But let us now proceed to consider,

II. What the Commandment before us, by Consequence, requires. And,

[o] Jer. xvii. 11. [p] Isa. lxv. 20. [q] 1 Cor. vi. 9.
[r] 1 Thess. iv. 6.

1. It

LECTURE XXVI.

1. It requires Restitution of whatever we have, at any Time, unjustly taken or detained. For, that being in Right not our own, but another's; keeping it is continuing and carrying on the Injustice. Therefore the Prophet *Ezekiel* makes it an express Condition of Forgiveness: *If the Wicked restore the Pledge, and give again that he had robbed; then he shall surely live, he shall not die*[s]. Nor was it till *Zaccheus* had engaged to restore amply what he had extorted from any one, that our Saviour declared, *This Day is Salvation come to this House*[t]. So that to think of raising Wealth by Fraud, and then growing honest, is the silliest Scheme in the World: for till we have returned, or offered to return, as far as we can, all that we have gotten by Fraud, we are not honest. Nay, suppose we have spent and squandered it, still we remain Debtors for it. Nay, suppose we got nothing, suppose we meant to get nothing, by any wicked Contrivances, in which we have been concerned; yet if we have caused another's Loss, any Loss for which Money is

[s] Ezek. xxxiii. 15. [t] Luke xix. 8, 9.

a proper Compensation; what we ought never to have done, we ought to undo as soon and as completely as we are able, however we straighten ourselves by it; otherwise we come short of making the Amends, which may justly be expected from us: and while so important a Part of Repentance is wanting, to demonstrate the Sincerity of the rest, we cannot hope to be accepted with God.

2. This Commandment also requires Industry: without which, the Generality of Persons cannot maintain themselves honestly. Therefore St. *Paul* directs: *Let him that stole, steal no more: but rather let him* (and certainly, by Consequence, every one else that needs) *labour, working with his Hands the Thing which is good* [u]. And each of them is to labour, not only for himself, but his Family also, if he hath one: both for their present, and, if possible, their future, Maintenance, in Case of Sickness, Accidents, or old Age. For as they, who belong to him, have, both by Nature and by Law, a Claim to Support from him, if they need it, and

[u] Eph. iv. 28.

LECTURE XXVI.

he can give it; neglecting to make due Provision for them is wronging them; and throwing either them or himself upon others, when he may avoid it, or however might have avoided it by proper Diligence, is wronging others. For which Reason the same Apostle *commanded* likewise, *that if any one would not work, neither should he eat* ʳ.

In order to be just therefore, be industrious: and doubt not but you will find it, after a while at least, by much the most comfortable, as well as Christian, Way of getting a Livelihood. It is a Way, that no one ought to think beneath him. For *better is he that laboureth, and aboundeth in all Things, than he that boasteth himself, and wanteth Bread* ˢ. It is the best Preservative that can be, from bad Company and bad Courses. It procures the good Will and good Word of Mankind. It exempts persons from the Contempt and Reproach of which those have bitter Experience, who make a dependent State their Choice. *Begging is sweet in the Mouth of the Shameless: but in his Belly there shall burn a Fire* ᵗ.

ʳ 2 Thess. iii. 10.   ˢ Ecclus. x. 27.   ᵗ Ecclus. xi. 30.

Very

LECTURE XXVI.

Very different from this is the Case of the Industrious. Their Minds are at Ease: their Bodies are usually healthy: their Time is employed as they know it should: what they get, they enjoy with a good Conscience, and it wears well. Nor do only the Fruits of their Labour delight them: but even Labour itself becomes pleasant to them.

And though Persons of higher Condition are not bound to *work with their Hands*; yet they also must be diligent in other Ways: in the Business of their Offices and Professions; or, if they have none, yet in the Care of their Families and Affairs. Else the former will be ill-governed, wicked and miserable: and the latter soon run into such Disorder, as will almost force them, either to be unjust to their Creditors, and those for whom Nature binds them to provide; or to be guilty of mean and dishonourable Actions of more Kinds than one, to avoid these and other disagreeable Consequences of their Supineness. Besides, as the upper Part of the World are peculiarly destined by Providence to be in one

Way

LECTURE XXVI.

Way or another extensively useful in Society: such of them as are not, defraud it of the Service they owe it, and therefore break this Commandment. But,

3. To observe it well, Frugality must be joined with Industry: else it will all be Labour in vain. For unwise Expensiveness will dissipate whatever the utmost Diligence can acquire. But if Idleness be added to Extravagance, that brings on quick Ruin. And if Intemperance and Debauchery go along with them, the Case is then come to its Extremity. Every one therefore, who desires to approve himself honest, should be careful to live within the Bounds of his Income, so as to have something in Readiness against the Time of Inability and unforeseen Events. But they who have, or design to have Families, should endeavour to live a good Deal within those Bounds. And whoever spends upon himself, or throws away upon any other Person or Thing more than he can prudently afford, (whatever false Names of Praise, as Elegance, Generosity, Good-nature, may be given to this Indiscretion) will

will be led, before he is aware, to diftrefs himfelf, perhaps many more; and be too probably driven at laft to repair, as well as he can, by Wickednefs, the Breaches which he hath made by Folly.

4. This Commandment requires in the laft Place, that we neither deny ourfelves or thofe who belong to us, what is fit for our and their Station, which is one Kind of Robbery; nor omit to relieve the Poor according to our Ability, which is another Kind. For whatever we enjoy of worldly Plenty is given us in Truft, that we fhould take our own Share with Moderation, and diftribute out of the Remainder with Liberality. And as they, who have but little, will, moft or all of them, at one Time or another, find thofe who have lefs; very few, if any, are exempted from giving fome Alms. And whoever either penurioufly or thoughtlefsly neglects his proper Share of this Duty, is unjuft to his Maker, and his Fellow-Creatures too. For the *Good*, which God hath placed in our Hands for the Poor is undoubtedly, as the Scripture declares it, *their Due*. He hath given them

LECTURE XXVI.

no Right to seize it: but he hath bound us not to *withhold* [z] it from them.

And now, having finished the two Heads proposed, I shall only add, that by observing these Directions from a Principle of Christian Faith; and teaching all under our Care to observe them from the same; the Poor in this World may be *rich towards God* [a] : and the Rich may *treasure up in Store for themselves a good Foundation against the Time to come*, which will enable them to *lay hold on eternal Life* [b].

[z] Prov. iii. 27.   [a] Luke xii. 21.   [b] 1 Tim. vi. 19.

LECTURE XXVII.

The Ninth Commandment.

THE Ninth Commandment is, connected with every one of the four which precede it. For neither the Duties of Superiors and Inferiors, nor those amongst Equals, could be tolerably practised; neither the Lives of Men, nor their Happiness in the nearest Relation of Life, nor their Possessions and Properties could ever be secure; if they were left exposed to those Injuries of a licentious Tongue, which are here prohibited. This Commandment therefore was intended, partly to strengthen the foregoing ones; and partly also, to make Provision for every Person's just Character on its own Account, as well as for the Sake of Consequences. For, independently on these, we have by Nature (and with Reason) a great Concern about our Reputations.

tions. And therefore the Precept, *Thou shalt not bear false Witness against thy Neighbour*, is, in all Views, of much Importance.

The Crime, at which these Words principally and most expressly point, is, giving false Evidence in any Cause or Trial. And as, in such Cases, Evidence hath always been given upon Oath; this Commandment, so far, is the same with the Third: only there, Perjury is forbidden, as Impiety against God; here, as injurious to Men. Now we are guilty of this Sin, if, in bearing Witness, we affirm that we know or believe any Thing, which we do not; or deny that we know or believe any Thing, which we do; or either affirm or deny more positively, than we have good Grounds. Nay, if we only stifle, by our Silence, any Fact, which is material, though we are not examined particularly about it; still when we have sworn in general to speak the whole Truth, we bear false Witness, if we designedly avoid it; especially after being asked, if we are able to say any Thing besides, relative to the Point in Question. For hiding a Truth may as totally mislead

those

LECTURE XXVII.

those who are to judge, as telling an Untruth. Indeed, if by any Means whatever we disguise the real State of the Case, instead of relating it in the fairest and plainest Manner that we can, we evidently transgress the Intent of this Commandment. And by doing it, the good Name, the Property, the Livelihood, the Life of an innocent Person, may be taken away; the Advantages of Society defeated, nay, perverted into Mischiefs, and the very Bonds of it dissolved. Therefore the Rule of the Mosaic Law is: *If a false Witness rise up against any Man, and testify against his Brother that which is wrong; then shall ye do unto him, as he had thought to have done unto his Brother, and thine Eye shall not pity*[a]. With us indeed, the Punishment extends not so far. But however mild such Persons may find the Penalties of human Laws to be, or how artfully soever they may evade them; God hath declared: *A false Witness shall not be unpunished: and he that speaketh Lies, shall not escape*[b].

[a] Deut. xix. 16—21.   [b] Prov. xix. 5.

LECTURE XXVII.

The Commandment faith only, that we shall not bear falfe Witnefs *againft* our Neighbour: but in Effect it binds us equally not to bear falfe Witnefs for him. For in all Trials of Property, bearing Witnefs for one Party is bearing Witnefs againft the other. And in all Trials for Crimes, falfe Evidence, to the Advantage of the Perfon accufed, is to the Difadvantage and Ruin of Right and Truth, of public Safety and Peace; by concealing and encouraging what ought to be detected and punifhed.

It being thus criminal to bear falfe Witnefs; it muft be criminal alfo to draw Perfons into the Commiffion of fo great a Sin, by Gifts or Promifes, or Threatenings, or any other Method. And, in its Degree, it muft be criminal to bring a falfe Accufation, or falfe Action againft any one; or to make any Sort of Demand, for which there is no reafonable Ground.

Nay further, however favourable Perfons are apt to think of the Defendant's Side; yet to defend ourfelves againft Juftice, or even to delay it by unfair Methods, is very wicked. For it ought to take Place;

and

LECTURE XXVII.

and the sooner, the better. Still, both the Professors of the Law, and others, may unquestionably say and do, for a doubtful or a bad Cause, whatever can be said with Truth, or done with Equity: for otherwise it might be thought still worse than it is; and treated worse than it deserves. But if they do, in any Cause, what in Reason ought not to be done: if they use or suggest indirect Methods of defeating the Intent of Law; if, by false Colours and Glosses, by terrifying or confounding Witnesses, by calumniating or ridiculing the adverse Party, they endeavour to make Justice itself an Instrument for patronizing Injustice; this is *turning Judgment into Gall*, as the Scriptures expresses it, *and the Fruit of Righteousness into Hemlock* [c].

But in a still higher Degree is it so, if Judges or Jurymen are influenced, in giving their Sentence or Verdict, by Interest, Relation, Friendship, Hatred, Compassion, Party; by any Thing, but the Nature of the Case, as it fairly appears to them. For designedly

[c] Amos vi. 12.

LECTURE XXVII.

making a false Determination, is completing all the Mischief, which bearing false Witness only attempts. And, in a Word, whoever any Way promotes what is wrong, or obstructs what is right, partakes in the same Sin: be it either of the Parties, their Evidences or Agents: be it the highest Magistrate, or the lowest Officer.

But Persons may break this Commandment, not only in judicial Proceedings; but, often full as grievously, in common Discourse: by raising, spreading, or countenancing false Reports against others; or such, as they have no sufficient Cause to think true; which is the Case, in Part at least, of most Reports: by misrepresenting their Circumstances in the World to their Prejudice; or speaking, without Foundation, to the Disadvantage of their Persons, Understandings, Accomplishments, Temper, or Conduct; whether charging them with Faults and Imperfections, which do not belong to them; or taking from them good Qualities and Recommendations, which do; or aggravating the former, or diminishing the latter: determining their Characters

from

LECTURE XXVII.

from a single bad Action or two; fixing ill Names on Things, which are really virtuous or innocent in them; imputing their laudable Behaviour to blameable or worthless Motives: making no Allowance for the Depravity or Weakness of human Nature, Strength of Temptation, Want of Instruction, wicked Insinuations, vicious Examples. And in all these Ways, Persons may be injured, either by open public Assertions; or more dangerously perhaps, by secret Whispers, which they have no Opportunity of contradicting. The Scandal may be accompanied with strong Expressions of hoping it is not true, or being very sorry for it; and warm Declarations of great good Will to the Party, whom it concerns; all which may serve only to give it a more unsuspected Credit. Nay, it may be conveyed very effectually in dark Hints, expressive Gestures, or even affected Silence. And these, as they may be equally mischievous, are not less wicked, for being more cowardly and more artful Methods of Defamation.

Further yet: Speaking or intimating Things to any Person's Disadvantage, though they

LECTURE XXVII.

they be true, is seldom innocent. For it usually proceeds from bad Principles: Revenge, Envy, Malice, Pride, Censoriousness; unfair Zeal for some private or Party Interest; or at best, from Desire of appearing to know more than others, or mere impertinent Fondness of talking. Now these are wretched Motives for publishing what will be hurtful to one of our Brethren. Sometimes indeed bad Characters and bad Actions ought to be known: but much oftener not, or not to all the World, or not by our Means. And we have Need to be very careful from what Inducements we act in such a Case. Sometimes again Things are known already; or soon will be known, let us be ever so silent about them: and then to be sure, we are more at Liberty. But even then, to take Pleasure in relating the Faults of others is by no Means right. And to reveal them, when they can be hid, unless a very considerable Reason require it, is extremely wrong.

Indeed we should be cautious, not only what Harm, but what Good we say of others. For speaking too highly of their

Characters

LECTURE XXVII.

Characters or Circumstances, or praising them in any Respect beyond Truth, is *bearing false Witness* about them: which may sometimes turn against them: and may often mislead those, to whom we exalt them thus; and produce grievously bad Consequences of many Kinds. But the other is much the more common, and usually the more hurtful, Extreme.

We all think it an Injury, in the tenderest Part, when bad Impressions are made on others concerning us; and therefore should conscientiously avoid doing the same Injury to others. Making them designedly, without Cause is inexcusable Wickedness. And even where we intend no Harm, we may do a great deal. Whatever hurts, in any Respect, the Reputation of Persons, always gives them great Pain, and often doth them great Prejudice, even in their most important Concerns. For indeed almost every Thing in this World depends on Character. And when once that hath suffered an Imputation; for the most Part, neither the Persons calumniated, be they ever so innocent, can recover it completely by their own

own Endeavours, nor the Persons who have wronged them, be they ever so desirous, restore it fully to its former State, though certainly they, who rob others of their good Name, or even without Design asperse it, are full as much bound to make Restitution for that, as for any other Damage, which they cause. But were they not to hurt at all the Person against whom they speak, still they hurt themselves, and lessen their Power of doing Good in the World; they often hurt their innocent Families by the Provocations which they give; they grieve their Friends; they set a mischievous Example in Society; and, if they profess any Religion, bring a dreadful Reproach upon it, by a Temper and Behaviour so justly hateful to Mankind.

It will easily be understood, that, next to the Raisers and Spreaders of ill Reports, they who encourage Persons of that Kind, by hearkening to them with Pleasure, and by Readiness of Belief in what they say, contradict the Intention of this Commandment. Indeed we ought, far from countenancing Scandal and Detraction, to express,

LECTURE XXVII.

press, in all proper Ways, our Dislike of it; shew the Uncertainty, the Improbability, the Falsehood, if we can, of injurious Rumours; oppose the divulging even of Truths that are uncharitable; and set a Pattern of giving every one his just Praise.

It must now be observed further, that though undoubtedly those Falsehoods are the worst, which hurt others the most directly, yet Falsehoods in general are hurtful and wrong. And therefore Lying; all Use either of Words or Actions of known settled Import, with Purpose to deceive; is unlawful. And those Offences of this Kind, which may seem the most harmless, have yet commonly great Evil in them. Lying destroys the very End of Speech, and leads us into perpetual Mistakes, by the very Means which God intended should lead us into Truth. It puts an End to all the Pleasure, all the Benefit, all the Safety of Conversation. Nobody can know, on what or whom to depend. For if one Person may lie, why not another? and at this Rate, no Justice can be done, no Wickedness be prevented or punished, no Business

go

go forward. All these Mischiefs will equally follow, whether Untruths be told in a gross barefaced Manner, or disguised under Equivocations, Quibbles, and Evasions. The Sin therefore is as great in one Case as the other. And it is so great in both, that no sufficient Excuses can ever be made for it in either, though several are often pleaded.

Many Persons imagine, that, when they have committed a Fault, it is very pardonable to conceal it under a Lie. But some Faults ought not to be concealed at all; and none by this Method; which is committing two, instead of one; and the second not uncommonly worse than the first. An ingenuous Confession will be likely, in most Cases, to procure an easy Pardon: but a Lie is a monstrous Aggravation of an Offence; and persisting in a Lie can very hardly be forgiven. But above all, if any Persons, to hide what they have done amiss themselves, are so vile as to throw the Blame or the Suspicion of it upon another; this is the Height of Wickedness. And therefore particularly all Children and Servants, who are

chiefly

LECTURE XXVII.

chiefly tempted to excuse themselves by telling Falsehoods, ought to undergo any Thing rather than be guilty of such a Sin. And on the other Hand, all Parents, Masters, and Mistresses, ought to beware of punishing them too severely for their other Offences; left they drive them into a Habit of this terrible one.

Some again plead for making free with Truth, that they do it only in Jest. But these Jests of theirs often occasion great Uneasiness and Disquiet; and sometimes other very serious bad Consequences. The Scripture therefore hath passed a severe Censure upon them. *As a Madman, who casteth Fire-Brands, Arrows, and Death; so is the Man that deceiveth his Neighbour, and saith, Am I not in Sport*[d]? To give another Person Vexation, or make him appear contemptible, though in a slight Instance, is by no Means innocent Sport. And besides, to speak Falsehood on any Occasion is a dangerous Introduction to speaking it on more, if not all, Occasions. For if so trifling a Motive as a Jest will prevail on us

[d] Prov. xxvi. 19.

to violate Truth, how can we be expected to withstand more weighty Temptations?

However, it may perhaps at least be thought, that lying, to prevent Mischief and do good, must be permitted. But the Scripture expresly forbids us to *do Evil, that Good may come*[c]. And they, who allow themselves in it, will usually be discovered and lose their End: or, if not, will never know where to stop. They will be enticed by Degrees to think every Thing good, that serves their Turn, let others think it ever so bad: those others again will think themselves authorized by such Example, to take the same Liberties: and thus all Trust and Probity will be lost amongst Men: a much greater Evil, than any Good, which Falsehood may do now and then, will ever compensate.

And if telling Lies, even from these plausible Inducements, be so bad; what must it be, when they proceed from less excusable ones, as Desire of promoting our own Interest, or that of our Party: and how completely detestable, when we are prompt-

[c] Rom. iii. 8.

ed

LECTURE XXVII.

ed to them by Malice, or undue Resentment, or any other totally wicked Principle!

Nor is the Practice less imprudent, than it is unlawful. Some indeed lie to raise their Characters, as others do to gain their Points. But both act very absurdly. For they miss of their Purpose entirely, as soon as they are found out: and all Lyars are found out; immediately, for the most Part; but in a while without Fail. And after that, every body despises and hates them: even when they speak Truth, nobody knows how to credit them: and so, by aiming wickedly at some little Advantage for the present, they put themselves foolishly under the greatest Disadvantage in the World ever after. *The Lip of Truth shall be established for ever: but a lying Tongue is but for a Moment* [f]. Beware then of the least Beginning of a Practice that will be sure to end ill. For if you venture upon Falsehood at all, it will grow upon you, and entangle you; and bring you to Shame, to Punishment, to Ruin. And, besides what you

[f] Prov. xii. 19, 22.

LECTURE XXVII.

will suffer by it here, your Portion, unless you repent very deeply, and amend very thoroughly, will be with the Father of Lies hereafter. For *into* the heavenly *Jerusalem shall in no Wise enter whosoever worketh Abomination, or maketh a Lie* [g]. *Lying Lips are Abomination to the Lord: but they, that deal truly, are his Delight* [h].

There is yet another Sort of Falsehood, often full as bad as affirming what we do not think: I mean, promising what we do not intend; or what we neglect afterwards to perform, so soon, or so fully, as we ought. Whoever hath promised, hath made himself a Debtor: and, unless he be punctual in his Payment, commits an Injustice; which in many Cases may be of very pernicious Consequence.

Now in order to secure this great Point of speaking Truth: besides considering carefully and frequently the before-mentioned Evils of departing from it, we should be attentive also to moderate the Quantity of our Discourse, lest we fall into Falsehood unawares. For *in the Multitude of Words*

[g] Rev. xxi. 27.   [h] Prov. xii. 22.

there

LECTURE XXVII.

there wanteth not Sin: but he that refraineth his Lips, is wife [i]. Perfons, who fuffer themfelves to run on heedlefsly in Talk, juft as their prefent Humour difpofes them, or the prefent Company will be beft pleafed; or who will fay almoft any Thing, rather than fay nothing; muft be perpetually tranfgreffing fome of the Duties comprehended under this Commandment; which yet it is of the utmoft Importance not to tranfgrefs. For, with Refpect to the Concerns of this World, *He that loveth Life, and would fee good Days, let him refrain his Tongue from Evil; and his Lips, that they fpeak no Guile* [k]. And, as to our eternal State in the next, *If any Man feem to be religious, and bridleth not his Tongue, that Man's Religion is vain* [l].

[i] Prov. x. 19.   [k] Pf. xxxiv. 12, 13.   [l] Jam. i. 26.

LECTURE

LECTURE XXVIII.

The Tenth Commandment.

WE are now come to the tenth and laſt Commandment; which is by the Church of *Rome* abſurdly divided into two, to keep up the Number, after joining the firſt and ſecond into one, contrary to ancient Authority, Jewiſh and Chriſtian. How the Miſtake was originally made, is hard to ſay: but undoubtedly they retain and defend it the more earneſtly, in order to paſs over the ſecond Commandment, as only Part of the firſt, without any diſtinct Meaning of its own. And accordingly many of their devotional Books omit it entirely. But that theſe two ought not to be thus joined and confounded, I have ſhewn you already. And that this, now before us, ought not to be divided, is extremely evident: for it is one ſingle Prohibition of all unjuſt

LECTURE XXVIII.

unjuſt Deſires. And if reckoning up the ſeveral prohibited Objects of Deſire makes it more than one Commandment; for the ſame Reaſon it will be more than two. For there are ſix Things forbidden in it particularly, beſides all the reſt, that are forbidden in general. And, moreover, if this be two Commandments, which is the firſt of them? For in *Exodus* it begins, *Thou ſhalt not covet thy Neighbour's Houſe:* but in Deuteronomy, *Thou ſhalt not covet thy Neighbour's Wife.* And accordingly ſome of their Books of Devotion make the former, ſome the latter of theſe, the ninth[a]. Surely the Order of the Words would never have been changed thus in Scripture, had there been two Commandments in them[b]: but

[a] Their Manual of Prayers in Engliſh, 1725, puts, *Thou ſhalt not covet thy Neighbour's Wife*, for the Ninth. But, in the Office of the Virgin, both Latin and Engliſh, called the Primer, 1717, *Thou ſhalt not covet thy Neighbour's Houſe*, is the Ninth.

[b] Indeed the Vatican Copy of the Septuagint in Exodus places, *Thou ſhalt not commit Adultery*, before *Thou ſhalt do no Murder*. And ſo do Mark x. 19. Luke xviii. 20. Rom. xiii. 9. and Philo, and Part of the Fathers. But the Hebrew and Samaritan, and all Tranſlations, excepting the Septuagint,

and

but being one, it is no way material, which Part is named first. I say no more therefore on so clear a Point: but proceed to explain this Precept, of *not coveting what is our Neighbour's.*

The good Things of this Life being the Gifts of God, for which all are to be thankful to him; desiring, with due Moderation and Submission, a comfortable Share of them, is very natural and right. Wishing, that our Share were better, is, in the Case of many Persons, so far from a Sin, that endeavouring diligently to make it better is Part of their Duty. Wishing it were equal to that of such another, is not wishing ill to him, but only well to ourselves. And seeking to obtain what belongs to another may, in proper Circumstances, be perfectly innocent. We may really have Occasion for it; he may be well able to bestow it; or he may have Occasion

and even That in Deuteronomy, and I believe most Copies of it in Exodus, and Matth. xix. 18. and Josephus, and another Part of the Fathers, keep the now common Order. And the Evangelists did not intend to observe the original Order: for they put, *Honour thy Father,* &c. last. And St. Paul doth not say, that he intended to observe it. This therefore is not a parallel Case to that of the Tenth Commandment.

for something of ours in Return. And on these mutual Wants of Men all Commerce and Trade is founded: which God, without Question, designed should be carried on; because he hath made all Countries abound in some Things, and left them deficient in others.

Not every Sort of Desires therefore, but unfit and immoderate Desires only, are forbidden by the Words, *Thou shalt not covet*. And these are such as follow. First, If our Neighbour cannot lawfully part with his Property, nor we lawfully receive it: and yet we want to have it. One Instance of this Kind is expressed, *Thou shalt not covet thy Neighbour's Wife*. Another is, if we want a Person who possesses any Thing in Trust, or under certain Limitations, to give or sell it in Breach of that Trust or those Limitations. Or if he can part with it, but is not willing; and we entertain Thoughts of acquiring it by Force or Fraud; or of being revenged on him for his Refusal; this also is highly blameable: for why should not he be left quietly free Master of his own? Indeed barely pressing and importuning Persons, contrary to their Interest,

or

or even their Inclinations only, is in some Degree wrong: for it is one Way of extorting Things from them; or however, of giving them Trouble, where we have no Right to give it.

But though we keep our Desires ever so much to ourselves, they may notwithstanding be very sinful. And such they are particularly, if they induce us to envy others: that is, to be uneasy at their imagined superior Happiness, to wish them ill, or take Pleasure in any Harm which befalls them. For this Turn of Mind will prompt us to do them ill, if we can: as indeed a great Part of the Mischief that is done in the World, and some of the worst of it, arises from hence. *Wrath is cruel, and Anger is outrageous: but who is able to stand against Envy*[c]? Accordingly we find it joined in the New Testament with *Strife, Railing, Variance, Sedition, Murder, Confusion, and every evil Work*[d]. But were it to produce no Mischief to our Neighbour, yet it is the

[c] Prov. xxii. 4.
[d] Rom. i. 29. xiii. 13. 1 Cor. iii. 3. 2 Cor. xii. 20. Gal. v. 20, 21. 1 Tim. vi. 4. Jam. iii. 14, 16.

directly opposite Disposition to that Love of him, which is the second great Precept of Christ's Religion. Nay indeed it deserves, in some Respects, to be reckoned the worst of ill-natured Sins. The revengeful Man pleads for himself some Injury attempted against him: but the envious Person bears unprovoked Malice to those, who have done him neither Wrong nor Harm, solely because he fancies them to be, in this or that Instance, very happy. And why should they not, if they can; as he certainly would, if he could? For the Prosperity of bad People, it must be confessed, we have Reason to be so far sorry, as they are likely to do Hurt by it. But to desire their Fall, rather than their Amendment; to desire what may be grievous to any Persons, not from good Will to Mankind, but from ill Will to them; to wish any Misfortune even to our Competitors and Rivals, merely because they are such; or because they have succeeded, and enjoy what we aimed at; is extremely uncharitable and inhuman. It is a Temper that will give us perpetual Disquiet in this World, (for there will always be somebody

body to envy) and bring a heavy Sentence upon us in the next, unless we repent of it, and subdue it first.

But though our selfish Desires were to raise in us no Malignity against our Fellow-Creatures; yet if they tempt us to murmur against our Creator; and either to speak or think ill of that Distribution of Things, which his Providence hath made; this is great Impiety, and Rebellion of the Heart against God: who hath an absolute Right to dispose of the Works of his Hands as He pleases; and uses it always both with Justice and with Goodness to us. Were we innocent, we could none of us demand more Advantages of any Sort, than He thought fit to give us: but as we are guilty Wretches; far from having a Claim to this or that Degree of Happiness, we are every one liable to severe Punishment. And therefore, with the many Comforts and Blessings which we have now, and the eternal Felicity which, through the Mercy of our heavenly Father, the Merits of our blessed Redeemer, and the Grace of the Holy Spirit, we may, if we will, have hereafter; surely, we have no

LECTURE XXVIII.

Ground to complain of our Condition. For what if Things be unequally divided here? We may be certain the Difpofer of them hath wife Reafons for it, whether we can fee them or not: and we may be as certain, that, unlefs it be our own Fault, we fhall be no Lofers by it: for *all Things work together for Good to them that love God*[e]. Therefore, how little foever we enjoy, we have Caufe to be thankful for it: and how much foever we fuffer, we have Caufe to be refigned; nay thankful too, even for that; as we may be happier in this world for many of our fufferings; and fhall, if we bear them as we ought, be improved in Goodnefs by them all, and made happier to Eternity.

But further yet: though we may not be confcious of what we fhall ftudy to hide from ourfelves, that our Defires carry us, either to behave or wifh ill to our Neighbours, or to repine againft God: ftill, if they difturb and agitate our Minds; if we are eager and vehement about the Objects of them; we are not arrived at the State, in

[e] Rom. viii. 28.

which

LECTURE XXVIII.

which we should be found. Some Feeling of this inward Tumult, especially on trying Occasions, may be unavoidable by fallen Man; and more of it natural to one Person than another: but after all, it is voluntary Indulgence, that gives our Appetites, and Passions, and Fancies, the far greatest Share of their Dominion. We inflame them, when else they would be moderate: we affect Things, for which we have really no Liking, merely because they are fashionable: we create imaginary Wants to ourselves; and then grow as earnest for what we might do perfectly well without, as if the whole of our Felicity consisted in it. This is a very immoral State of Mind: and hurries Persons, almost irresistibly, into as immoral a Course of Life. In Proportion as worldly Inclinations of any Kind engage the Heart, they exclude from it social Affection, Compassion, Generosity, Integrity; and yet more effectually Love to God, and Attention to the Concerns of our future State. Nor do they almost ever fail to make us at present miserable, as well as wicked. They prey upon our Spirits, torment us

with

with perpetual Self-Diſlike, waſte our Health, ſink our Character, drive us into a thouſand fooliſh Actions to gratify them; and, when all is done, can never be gratified, ſo as to give us any laſting Satisfaction. Firſt, we ſhall be full of Anxieties and Fears: when we have got over theſe and obtained our Wiſh, we ſhall quickly find it comes very ſhort of our Expectation: then we ſhall be cloyed, and tired, and wretchedly languid, till ſome new Craving ſets us on Work to as little Purpoſe as the former did; or till we are wiſe enough to ſee, that ſuch Purſuits are not the Way to Happineſs.

But ſuppoſing Perſons are not violent in purſuing the imagined good Things of this World; yet if they be dejected and grieved, that no more of them have fallen to their Lot; if they mourn over the Inferiority of their Condition, and live in a perpetual Feeling of Affliction (be it ever ſo calm) on that Account; or indeed on Account of any Croſs or Diſadvantage whatever, belonging to the preſent Life: this alſo is a Degree, though the loweſt and leaſt, yet ſtill a Degree, of inordinate Deſire. For we are not grateful,

LECTURE XXVIII.

grateful, if, inftead of taking our Portion of Happinefs here with Chearfulnefs, and due Acknowledgments for it, we only lament that it is not, in this or that Refpect, more confiderable; and we are not wife, if we embitter it, be it ever fo fmall, by a fruitlefs Sorrow, inftead of making the beft of it.

Thefe then being the Exceffes, which this Commandment forbids; the Duty, which of Courfe it requires, is, that we *learn*, like St. *Paul, in whatfoever State we are, therewith to be content* [f]. This Virtue every body practifes in fome Cafes: for who is there, that could not mention feveral Things which he fhould be glad to have, yet is perfectly well fatisfied to go without them? And would we but ftrive to be of the fame Difpofition in all Cafes; the Self-Enjoyment, that we fhould reap from it, is inexpreffible. The worldly Condition of Multitudes is really quite as good as it needs to be; and of many others (who do not think fo) as good as it well can be. Now for fuch to be anxious about mending it, is

[f] Phil. iv. 11.

only

LECTURE XXVIII.

only being miserable for nothing. And in whatever we may have Cause to wish our Circumstances were better, moderate Wishes will be sufficient to excite a reasonable Industry to improve them, as far as we can: and immoderate Eagerness will give us no Assistance, but only Disquiet. More than a few consume themselves with longing for what Indolence and Despondency will not suffer them to try if they can obtain. *The Desire of the Slothful killeth him: for his Hands refuse to labour* [r]. And sometimes, on the contrary, the Precipitance, with which we aim at a favourite Point, is the very Reason that we overshoot the Mark, and miss it.

But supposing the most solicitous were always the most likely to gain their Ends: yet this Likelihood will be often crossed, both by Delays and Disappointments; which to impatient Tempers will be extremely grievous: and the saddest Disappointment of all will be, that they will find the most perfect Accomplishment of their Wishes, after a very small Time, to be little or no Increase of their Happiness. Persons un-

[r] Prov. xxi. 25.

easy

easy in their present Situation, or intent on some darling Object, imagine that could they but succeed in such a Pursuit, or had they but such a Person's good Fortune or Accomplishments, then they should be perfectly at Ease, and lastingly delighted. But they utterly mistake. Every Enjoyment palls and deadens quickly: every Condition hath its unseen Inconveniencies and Sufferings, as wells as its visible Advantages. And Happiness depends scarce at all on the Preeminence commonly admired. For the Noble, the Powerful, the Rich, the Learned, the Ingenious, the Beautiful, the Gay, the Voluptuous, are usually to the full as far from it, and by Turns own they are, as any of the Wretches, whom they severally despise. Indeed, when every Thing is tried round, we shall experience at last, what we had much better see at first, as we easily may, that the cheerful Composure of a reasonable and religious, and therefore contented, Mind, is the only solid Felicity that this World affords; the great Blessing of Heaven here below; that will enable us to relish the rest, if we have them; and to be

satisfied,

satisfied, if we have them not. What *Solomon* hath said of Wealth, he found to be equally true of every Thing else beneath the Sun. *God giveth to a Man, that is good in his Sight, Wisdom, and Knowledge, and Joy: but to the Sinner he giveth Travel, to gather and heap up.—This also is Vanity, and Vexation of Spirit* [h].

Contentment therefore being the Gift of God, we should earnestly pray to Him for it. And in order to become fit Objects of his Favour, we should frequently and thankfully recollect the many undeserved Comforts of our Condition, that we may bear the Afflictions of it more patiently; reasoning with *Job, Shall we receive Good at the Hand of God, and shall we not receive Evil* [i] ? Nor should we fail to join with our Meditations on his past and present Mercies, the firm Assurance, which both his Attributes and his Promises furnish, that the same *loving Kindness shall follow us all the Days of our Life* [k]; and be exerted, though sometimes for our Correction or Trial, yet always for our Benefit; and so as to make

[h] Eccl. ii. 26.   [i] Job ii. 10.   [k] Psalm xxiii. 6.

LECTURE XXVIII.

our Lot fupportable in every Variety of outward Circumftances. *Let your Converfation therefore be without Covetoufnefs; and be content with fuch Things as ye have: for He hath faid, I will never leave thee, nor forfake thee* [1]. Another very important Confideration, and neceffary to be often brought to Mind, is, that the Seafon both of enjoying the Advantages, and bearing the Inconveniences, of Life is fhort: but the Reward of enjoying and bearing each, as we ought, is eternal and inconceivably great.

Together with thefe Reflections, let us exercife a fteady Care to check every faulty Inclination in its earlieft Rife. For it is chiefly indulging them at firft, that makes them fo hard to conquer afterwards. And yet we fhall always find the bad Confequences of yielding to outweigh vaftly the Trouble of refifting: and that to bring our Defires, when they are the ftrongeft, down to our Condition, is a much eafier Work, than to raife our Condition up to our Defires, which will only grow the more ungovernable, the more they are pampered.

[1] Heb. xiii. 5.

Further:

LECTURE XXVIII.

Further: whatever Share we possess of wordly Plenty, let us bestow it on ourselves with decent Moderation, and impart of it to others with prudent Liberality: for thus *knowing how to abound*, we shall *know* the better *how to suffer Need* [m], if Providence calls us to it. And lastly, instead of *setting our Affections on* any *Things on Earth* [n], which would be a fatal Neglect of the great End, that we are made for, let us exalt our Views to that blessed Place, where *Godliness with Contentment will be* unspeakable *Gain* [o]: and they who have restrained the inferior Principles of their Nature by the Rules of Religion, shall have the highest Faculties of their Souls *abundantly satisfied with the Fatness of God's House, and be made to drink of the River of his Pleasures* [p].

Thus then you see both the Meaning, and the Importance, of this last Commandment: which is indeed the Guard and Security of all the preceding ones. For our Actions will never be right habitually,

[m] Phil. iv. 12.   [n] Col. iii. 2.   [o] 1 Tim. vi. 6.
[p] Psalm xxxvi. 8.

till

LECTURE XXVIII.

till our Desires are so. Or if they could; our Maker demands the whole Man, as he surely well may: nor, till that is devoted to Him, are we *meet for the Inheritance of the Saints in Light* q.

And now, both the first and the second Table of the Ten Commandments having been explained to you, it only remains, that we beg of God *sufficient grace*ʳ to keep them; earnestly entreating him in the Words of his Church: *Lord, have Mercy upon us, and write all these thy Laws in our Hearts, we beseech thee.*

q Col. i. 12.   r 2 Cor. xii. 9.

LECTURE XXIX.

Of Man's Inability, God's Grace, and Prayer to Him for it.

I HAVE now proceeded, in the Course of these Lectures to the End of the Commandments; and explained the Nature of that Repentance, Faith and Obedience, which were promised for us in our Baptism, and which we are bound to exercise, in Proportion as we come to understand the Obligations incumbent on us. You cannot but see by this Time, that the Duties, which God injoins us, are not only very important, but very extensive. And therefore a Consideration will almost unavoidably present itself to your Minds in the next Place, what Abilities we have to perform them. Now this Question our Catechism decides, without asking it, by a Declaration, extremely discouraging in Appearance;

pearance; that *we are not able, of ourselves, to walk in the Commandments of God, and to serve him.*

Indeed, had we ever so great Abilities, we must have them, not of ourselves, but of our Maker; from whom all the Powers of all Creatures are derived. But something further than this, is plainly meant here: that there are no Powers, belonging to human Nature in its present State, sufficient for so great a Purpose. *The Law of God is spiritual, but we are carnal, sold under Sin*[a]. And that such is our Condition, will appear by reflecting, first, what it was at our Birth; secondly, what we have made it since.

1. As to the first: we all give Proofs, greater or less, of an inbred Disorder and Wrongness in our Understandings, Will, and Affections. Possibly one Proof, that some may give of it, may be a Backwardness to own it. But they little consider, how severe a Sentence they would pass, by denying it, on themselves, and all Mankind. Even with our natural bad Incli-

[a] Rom. vii. 14.

LECTURE XXIX.

nations for some Excuse, we are blameable enough for the ill Things that we do. But how much more should we be so, if we did them all, without the Solicitation of any inward Depravity to plead afterwards in our Favour? In Point of Interest therefore, as well as Truth, we are concerned to admit an original Proneness to Evil in our Frame: while yet Reason plainly teaches, at the same Time, that whatever God created was originally, in its Kind, perfect and good.

To reconcile these two Things would have been a great Difficulty, had not Revelation pointed out the Way, by informing us, that *Man* was indeed *made upright*[b], but that the very first of human Race lost their Innocence and their Happiness together; and tainting, by wilful Transgression, their own Nature, tainted, by Consequence, that of their whole Posterity. Thus *by one Man, Sin entered into the World, and Death by Sin; and so Death passed upon all Men, for that all have sinned*[c]. We find in Fact, however difficult it may be to ac-

[b] Eccl. vii. 29.   [c] Rom. v. 12.

count for it in Speculation, that the Dispositions of Parents, both in Body and Mind, very commonly descend, in some Degree, to their Children. And therefore it is entirely credible, that so great a Change in the Minds of our first Parents from absolute Rightness of Temper to presumptuous Wickedness; accompanied with an equal Change of Body, from an immortal Condition to a mortal one, produced perhaps, in Part, by the physical Effects of the forbidden Fruit; that these Things, I say, should derive their fatal Influences to every succeeding Generation. For though God will never impute any Thing to us, as our personal Fault, which is not our own Doing; yet he may very justly withhold from us those Privileges, which he granted to our first Parents only on Condition of their faultless Obedience, and leave us subject to those Inconveniences, which followed of Course from their Disobedience: as, in Multitudes of other Cases, we see Children in far worse Circumstances by the Faults of their distant Forefathers, than they otherwise would have been. And most evidently

it

LECTURE XXIX.

it is no more a Hardship upon us, to become such as we are by Means of *Adam's* Transgression, than to suffer what we often do for the Transgressions of our other Ancestors; or to have been created such as we are, without any one's Transgression: which last, all, who disbelieve original Sin, must affirm to be our Case.

But unhappy for us as the Failure of the first Man was, we should be happy in Comparison, if this were all, that we had to lament. Great as the native Disorder of our Frame is; yet either the Fall of Adam left in it, or God restored to it, some Degree of Disposition to Obedience, and of Strength against Sin: so that though *in us, that is in our Flesh, dwelleth no good Thing*[d], yet *after the inward Man, (the Mind) we delight in the Law of God*[e]; and there are Occasions, on which even *the Gentiles, which have not the Law, do by Nature the Things contained in the Law*[f], though neither all, nor any, without Fault. And on us Christians our heavenly Father confers, in our Baptism, the Assurance of much greater Strength to obey his

[d] Rom. vii. 18.   [e] Ver. 22, 23.   [f] Rom. ii. 14.

Commands, than they have. But then, if we confider

2. What we have made our Condition fince, we fhall find, that inftead of ufing well the Abilities which we had, and taking the Methods, which our Maker hath appointed for the Increafe of them, we have often carelefsly, and too often wilfully, mifemployed the former, and neglected the latter. Now by every Inftance of fuch Behaviour, we difpleafe God, weaken our right Affections, and add new Strength to wrong Paffions: and by Habits of fuch Behaviour, corrupting our Hearts, and blinding our Underftandings, we bring ourfelves into a much worfe Condition, than that, in which we were born; and thus become doubly incapable of doing our Duty. This, Experience proves but too plainly; though Scripture did not teach, as it doth, that *the Imagination of Man's Heart is Evil from his Youth* [g]: that *we were fhapen in Iniquity, and in Sin did our Mother conceive us* [h]: that *the carnal Mind is Enmity againft God* [i]: that *without Chrift, we can do nothing* [k]; *and that*

[g] Gen. viii. 21.   [h] Pf. li. 5.   [i] Rom. viii. 7.   [k] John xv. 5.

LECTURE XXIX.

we are not sufficient to think any Thing, as of ourselves[1].

Yet, notwithstanding this, we feel within us an Obligation of Conscience to do every Thing that is right and good. For that Obligation is in its Nature unchangeable: and we cannot be made happy otherwise, than by endeavouring to fulfil it; though God, for the Sake of our blessed Redeemer, will make fit Allowances for our coming short of it. But then we must not hope for such Allowances as would really be unfit. Our original Weakness indeed is not our Fault: but our Neglect of being relieved from it, and the Additions that we have made to it, are. And whatever we might have had the Power of doing, if we would; it is no Injustice to punish us for not doing: especially when the Means of enabling ourselves continue to be offered to us through our Lives. Now, in Fact, the whole Race of Mankind, I charitably hope and believe, have, by the general Grace or Favour of God, the Means of doing so much, at least, as may exempt

[1] 2 Cor. iii. 5.

them from future Sufferings. But Christians, by the *special Grace* mentioned in this Part of the Catechism, are qualified to do so much more, as will intitle them, not for their own Worthiness, but that of the holy Jesus, to a distinguishing Share of future Reward.

Now the special Grace of the Gospel consists, partly in the outward Revelation, which it makes to us, of divine Truths; partly in the inward Assistance, which it bestows on us for obeying the divine Will. The latter is the Point, here to be considered.

That God is able, by secret Influences on our Minds, to dispose us powerfully in Favour of what is Right, there can be no Doubt: for we are able in some Degree to influence one another thus. That there is Need of his doing it, we have all but too much Experience: and that therefore we may reasonably hope for it, evidently follows. He interposes continually by his Providence, to carry on the Course of Nature in the material World: is it not then very likely, that he should interpose in a

Case,

LECTURE XXIX.

Cafe, which, as far as we can judge, is yet more worthy of his Interpofition; and incline and ftrengthen his poor Creatures to become good and happy, by gracious Impreffions on their Souls, as Occafions require? But ftill, Hope and Likelihood are not Certainty: and God, *whofe Ways are paft finding out* [m], might have left all Men to their own Strength, or rather indeed their own Weaknefs. But whatever he doth in Relation to others, which is not our Concern, he hath clearly promifed to us Chriftians, that *his Grace fhall be fufficient for us* [n]; his Holy Spirit fhall enable us effectually to do every Thing which his Word requires.

We may *refift* [o] his Motions: or we may receive them into our Souls, and act in confequence of them. Every one hath Power enough to do right: Scripture, as well as Reafon, fhews it: only we have it not refident in us by Nature; but beftowed on us continually by our Maker, as we want it. In all good Actions that we perform, *the Preparation of the Heart is from the Lord* [p]. And

[m] Rom. xi. 33. [n] 2 Cor. xii. 9. [o] Acts vii. 51. [p] Prov. xvi. 1.

that *Faith*, which is the Fountain of all Actions truly good, *is not of ourselves, it is the Gift of God*[q]. But *he giveth liberally to all*[r], who ask him; and therefore no one hath Cause of Complaint.

It is true, we are seldom able to distinguish this heavenly Influence from the natural Workings of our own Minds: as indeed we are often influenced one by another without perceiving it. But the Assurance, given in Scripture, of its being vouchsafed to us, is abundantly sufficient: to which, Experience also would add strong Confirmation, did we but attend with due Seriousness to what passes within our Breasts.

Our natural Freedom of Will is no more impaired by these secret Admonitions of our Maker, than by the secret Persuasions of our Fellow-Creatures. And the Advantage of having God's Help, far from making it unnecessary to help ourselves, obliges us to it peculiarly. We are therefore to *work out our own Salvation*, because *He worketh in us both to will and to do*[s]. For it is a great Aggravation of every Sin, that, in committing

[q] Eph. ii. 8.   [r] James i. 5.   [s] Phil. ii. 12, 13.

LECTURE XXIX.

it, we *quench* the pious Motions excited by *the Spirit*[t] of God in our Hearts: and a great Incitement to our Endeavours of performing every Duty, that with such Aid we may be sure of Success. Our own natural Strength cannot increase, as Temptations and Difficulties do: but that, which we receive from Heaven, can. And thus it is that we learn Courage and Humility at once; by knowing, that *we can do all Things* but only *through Christ which strengtheneth us*[u]; and therefore *not we, but the Grace of God which is with us*[w].

This Grace therefore being of such Importance to us, our Catechism, with great Reason, directs us *at all Times to call for it by diligent Prayer*. For our heavenly Father hath not promised, nor can we hope, that He *will give the Holy Spirit to them who* proudly disdain, or negligently omit to *ask Him*[x]. And hence, it becomes peculiarly necessary, that we should understand how to pray to Him: a Duty mentioned in the former Part of the Catechism, but reserved to be explained more fully in this.

[t] 1 Thess. v. 19. [u] Phil. iv. 13. [w] 1 Cor. xv. 10.
[x] Luke xi. 13.

God

LECTURE XXIX.

God having bestowed on us the Knowledge, in some Measure, of what He is in Himself, and more especially of what He is to us; we are doubtless bound to be suitably affected by it: and to keep alive in our Minds, with the utmost Care, due Sentiments of our continual Dependance on Him, of Reverence and Submission to his Will, of Love and Gratitude for his Goodness, of Humility and Sorrow for all our Sins against Him; and earnest Desire, that his Mercy and Favour may be shewn, in such Manner as He shall think fit, to us and to all our Fellow-Creatures.

Now, if these Sentiments ought to be felt, they ought also to be some Way expressed: not only that others may see we have them, and be excited to them by our Example; but that we ourselves may receive both the Comfort and the Improvement, which must naturally flow from exercising such valuable Affections. And unquestionably the most lively and most respectful Manner of exercising them is, that we direct them to Him who is the Object of them; and pour out our Hearts before Him in suitable

LECTURE XXIX.

able Acts of Homage, Thankfgiving, and Confeſſion; in humble Petitions for ourſelves, and Interceſſions for all Mankind. Not that God is ignorant, till we inform Him, either of our outward Circumſtances, or the inward Temper of our Hearts. If He were, our Prayers would give Him but very imperfect Knowledge of either: for we are greatly ignorant of both ourſelves. But the Deſign of Prayer is, to bring our own Minds into a right Frame; and ſo make ourſelves fit for thoſe Bleſſings, for which we are very unfit, while we are too vain or too careleſs to aſk them of God.

The very Act of Prayer therefore will do us good, if we pray with Attention, elſe it is nothing; and with Sincerity, elſe it is worſe than nothing. And the Conſequences of praying, God hath promiſed, ſhall be further Good. *All things whatſoever ye ſhall aſk in Prayer, believing, ye ſhall receive*[y]. Not abſolutely *all Things whatſoever* we deſire: for ſome of our Deſires may be on ſeveral Accounts unfit, and ſome would prove extremely hurtful to us. Therefore

[y] Matth. xxi. 22.

we ought to consider well what we pray for: and especially in all temporal Matters refer ourselves wholly to God's good Pleasure. Nor doth he always grant immediately what He designs to grant, and hath given us the fullest Right to ask: but delays it perhaps a while to exercise our Patience and Trust in Him: for which Reason our Saviour directs us *always to pray, and not to faint*[z]. But whatever is really good, He will undoubtedly, as soon as it is really necessary, give us upon our Request: provided further, that with our earnest Petitions, we join our honest Endeavours: for Prayer was never designed to serve instead of Diligence, but to assist it. And therefore, if, in our temporal Affairs, we are idle or inconsiderate, we must not expect that our Prayers will bring us good Success: and if, in our spiritual ones, we wilfully or thoughtlessly neglect ourselves; we must not imagine, that God will amend us against our Wills, or whilst we continue supinely indifferent. But let us do our Duty to the best of our Power, at the same Time that

[z] Luke xviii. 1.

LECTURE XXIX.

we pray for his Blessing; and we may be assured, that nothing but an injurious Disbelief can prevent our obtaining it: on which Account St. *James* requires that we *ask in Faith, nothing wavering* [a].

Indeed without the Encouragement given us in Scripture, it might well be with some Diffidence, and it should still be with the utmost Reverence, that *we take upon us to speak unto the Lord, who are but Dust and Ashes* [b]. The Heathens therefore addressed their Prayers to imaginary Deities of an inferior Rank, as judging themselves unworthy to approach the supreme One. But our Rule is, *Thou shalt worship the Lord thy God, and Him only shalt thou serve* [c]. The affected *Humility of worshipping* even *Angels*, and therefore much more Saints, (who, if really such, are yet *lower than Angels* [d]) may, as we are taught, *beguile us of our Reward* [e]: whereas we may *come boldly to the Throne of* our Maker's *Grace* [f], though not in our own Right, yet through the Mediator whom he hath appointed: and

[a] Jam. i. 6. [b] Gen. xviii. 27. [c] Matth. iv. 10.
[d] Pf. viii. 5. [e] Col. ii. 18. [f] Heb. iv. 16.

who hath both procured us the Privilege; and inftructed us how to ufe it, by delivering to us a Prayer of his own Compofition; which might be at once a Form for us frequently to repeat, and a Pattern for us always to imitate.

That the Lord's Prayer was defigned as a Form, appears from his own Words: *After this Manner pray ye*; or, tranflating more literally, *Thus pray ye* [g]; and, which is yet more exprefs, *When ye pray, fay, Our Father* [h], &c. Befides it was given by Him to his Difciples on their Requeft, that He would *teach them to pray, as John alfo taught his Difciples* [i]: which undoubtedly was, as the great Rabbies amongft the *Jews* commonly taught theirs, by a Form. And accordingly this Prayer hath been confidered and ufed as fuch, from the earlieft Ages of Chriftianity down to the prefent.

Yet our Saviour's Defign was not, that this fhould be the only Prayer of Chriftians: as appears both from the Precepts and the Practice of the Apoftles, as well as from the Nature and Reafon of the Thing. But

[g] Matth. vi. 9.   [h] Luke xi. 2.   [i] Ver. 1.

when

LECTURE XXIX.

when it is not used as a Form, it is however of unspeakable Advantage as a Model. He proposes it indeed more particularly as an Example of Shortness. Not that we are never to make longer Prayers: for He himself *continued all Night in Prayer to God* [k]: and we have a much longer, made by the Apostles, in the fourth Chapter of the Acts. But his Intention was, to teach by this Instance, that we are not to affect unmeaning Repetitions, or any needless Multiplicity of Words, as if we *thought that we should be heard for our much speaking* [l]. And not only in this Respect, but every other, is our Lord's Prayer an admirable Institution and Direction for praying aright: as will abundantly appear, when the several Parts of it come to be distinctly explained. But though such Explanation will shew, both the Purport and the Excellency of it, more fully; yet they are to every Eye visible in the main, without any Explanation at all. And therefore let us conclude at present with devoutly offering it up to God.

[k] Luke vi. 12. [l] Matth. vi. 7.

LECTURE XXIX.

Our Father, which art in Heaven, hallowed be thy Name. Thy Kingdom come. Thy Will be done in Earth, as it is in Heaven. Give us this Day our daily Bread. And forgive us our Trespasses, as we forgive them that trespass against us. And lead us not into Temptation, but deliver us from Evil. For thine is the Kingdom, and the Power, and the Glory, for ever and ever. Amen.

LECTURE XXX.

The LORD's PRAYER.

Our Father, which art in Heaven, hallowed be thy Name.

THE Prayer which our blessed Saviour taught his Disciples, doth not need to be explained, as being, in itself, and originally, obscure. For no Words could be more intelligible to his Apostles, than all those, which he hath used throughout it. And even to Us now, there is nothing that deserves the Name of difficult; notwithstanding the Distance of Time, the Change of Circumstances, and the different Nature and Turn of the Jewish Tongue from our own. But still, in Order to apprehend it sufficiently, there is requisite

some

some Knowledge of Religion, and the Language of Religion. Besides, as we all learnt it when we were young, whilst we had but little Understanding, and less Attention; it is not impossible, but some of us may have gone on repeating it to an advanced Age, without considering it near so carefully, as we ought. And this very Thing, that the Words are so familiar to us, may have been the main Occasion, that we have scarce ever thought of their Import. Now we are sensible, it would be a great Unhappiness to have our Devotions, as the Church of *Rome* have the principal Part of theirs, in a Language that we could not understand. But surely it is as great a Fault, if, when we may so easily understand them, we do not; or if, though we do understand them, when we think of the Matter, we think about it so little, that, as to all good Purposes, it is much the same with praying in an unknown Tongue. The Lord's Prayer, in itself, is very clear, very expressive, very comprehensive. But all this is nothing to us, if we say it without knowing, or without minding, what we say. For how excellent Words soever we use;

if

LECTURE XXX.

if we add no Meaning to them, this can be no praying. And therefore, to make it really beneficial to us, we muſt fix deeply in our Thoughts what it was intended by its Author to contain.

Now it confiſts, you may obſerve, of three Parts. I. An Invocation, or calling upon God. II. Petitions offered. III. Praiſes aſcribed to Him.

The Invocation is in theſe Words, *Our Father, which art in Heaven*. And, few as they are, they expreſs very fully the Grounds on which Divine Worſhip ſtands.

As the whole World derives its Being from God, He is on that Account ſtiled, *the Father of all*[a]. But as rational Creatures are produced, not only by Him, but in his Image and Likeneſs, He is in a ſtricter Senſe the Father of theſe. And therefore Angels and Men are called in Scripture, what the Animals beneath them never are, *the Sons*[b], and the *Offspring of God*[c]: in which Senſe the Prophet ſaith, *O Lord, thou art our Father, and we are all*

[a] Eph. iv. 6. [b] Job i. 6. ii. 1. xxxviii. 7. [c] Acts xvii. 29.

LECTURE XXX.

the Work of thy Hand[d]. Now, as our Creator, he is evidently not only our Father, but also our sovereign Lord.

A second Title God hath to this Name, from that fatherly Providence and Goodness, which he exercises every where continually: and of which Mankind hath large Experience; not only in the many Enjoyments, Comforts, and Deliverances, that He grants us, but even in the Afflictions which He sends us, always for our Benefit; then more especially *dealing with us as with Children, whom he loveth*[e].

But there is yet a third Reason, why we call Him *our Father*, peculiar to us as Christians; and founded on our being united by Faith to his Son *our Head*[f], *and begotten again, through his Gospel, to a lively Hope, to an Inheritance reserved in Heaven for us*[g]: Privileges so invaluable, that though He is doubtless a Father, and a tender one, to our whole Species, yet his Word speaks of Us, as the only Persons, in Comparison, that have a Right to consider Him in this

[d] Isa. lxiv. 8. [e] Heb. xii. 5, &c. [f] 1 Cor. xi. 3.
Eph. i. 22. [g] 1 Cor. iv. 15. 1 Pet. i. 3, 4.

LECTURE XXX. 153

View. *As many as received Him*, that is our blessed Saviour, *to them gave He Power to become the Sons of God; even to them that believe on his Name*[h]. *The Lord is good to all*[i]: but singularly good to those, who become, by the Influences of the Christian Covenant, singularly fit Objects of his Goodness. They have Promises of the greatest Blessings, to which nothing, but Promise, can intitle: Pardon of Sin, Assistance of the Holy Spirit, and Life eternal; by which last they are made, in the happiest Sense, the *Children of God, being the Children of the Resurrection*[k]. Let us learn then, as often as we say, *Our Father*, to magnify in our Souls, that gracious Redeemer, who hath made Him so to us, more than He is to others. Let us often repeat the thankful Reflection of St. *John*, *Behold what Manner of Love the Father hath bestowed on us, that we should be called the Sons of God*[l]: and joyfully argue as St. *Paul* doth, *If Children, then Heirs; Heirs of God, and joint Heirs with Christ*[m].

[h] John i. 12. [i] Psalm cxlv. 9. [k] Luke xx. 36.
[l] 1 John iii. 1. [m] Rom. viii. 17.

Thus

LECTURE XXX.

Thus then the Words, *Our Father*, express, not only the absolute Authority, but the unspeakable Goodness of God: and the next, *which art in Heaven*, acknowledge his Glory and Power.

I have already observed to you, in explaining the sixth Article of the Creed, that as God cannot but be, so he cannot but be every where: for there is nothing in any one Part of Space to confine his Presence to that, rather than to any other. Besides, his Providence is continually acting every where: and wherever He acts, He is. Therefore Solomon justly declares, *The Heaven, and Heaven of Heavens cannot contain thee* [n]. But still the Scriptures represent Him as manifesting the more visible Tokens of his inexpressible Majesty in one peculiar Place: where He receives the Homage of his holy Angels, and issues forth his Commands for the Government of the World. This they call his *Throne* [o], and *Tabernacle in Heaven* [p]: of which the earthly Tabernacle of *Moses* was designed to be a Figure;

[n] 1 Kings viii. 27.   2 Chron. ii. 6. vi. 18.   [o] Pf. xi. 4.
[p] Heb. viii. 1, 2.

being

LECTURE XXX.

being directed to be *made according to the Pattern, shewed him in the Mount* [q]. That earthly Tabernacle was honoured for a long Time with splendid Marks of the Divine Residence: on which Account, even after they were withdrawn, the Jews would be apt to consider God, as dwelling at *Jerusalem* in his Temple, and *sitting between the Cherubim* [r]. But our blessed Lord, being about to abolish the Mosaic Ordinances, enlarges the Views of his Disciples, and raises them to that higher Habitation of inconceivable Glory, to which they should hereafter be admitted; and on which they were in the mean while to set their Hearts, as the seat of all Blessedness.

But further, being *in Heaven* denotes likewise the almighty Power of God: agreeably to that of the Psalmist, *Our God is in the Heavens: He hath done whatsoever He pleased* [s]. For as a higher Situation gives a superior Strength and Command; and accordingly in all Languages, being exalted or brought low, signifies an Increase or Lessening of Dominion or In-

[q] Heb. viii. 5.   [r] Psalm xcix. 1.   [s] Psalm cxv. 3.

fluence:

fluence: so representing God, as placed above all, is designed to express, in the strongest Manner, that *His Kingdom ruleth over all*[t].

When therefore we call upon *our Father which is* in Heaven, we profess to God our Belief, that He is the Author and Preserver of the Universe, who governs all Things with paternal Care; but extends his Favours especially to those, who by imitating and obeying Him shew themselves his true Children: and therefore most especially to such, as having acquired, by the Merits and Grace of his Son, the nearest Relation and Resemblance to Him, have thereby a Covenant-Right to an eternal Inheritance in that blessed Place, where He exhibits his Glory, and reigns, possessed of sovereign Authority, and boundless Power.

Now applying thus to God, under the Notion of *our Father*, is excellently fitted to remind us, both of the dutiful Regard, which we ought to have for him, as He himself pleads, *If I be a Father, where is*

[t] Psalm ciii. 19.

mine

LECTURE XXX.

mine Honour[n]; and also, of the Kindness, which we may expect from him, according to our Saviour's Reasoning, *If ye, being evil, know how to give good Gifts unto your Children; how much more shall your heavenly Father give his Holy Spirit to them that ask him*[w]? Nor is this Expression less fitted to admonish us of copying the Goodness, which we adore; and exercising Mercy and Bounty towards all our Fellow-Creatures, as far as we can, *that we may be,* in this excellent Sense, *the Children of our Father, which is in Heaven: for he maketh his Sun to rise on the Evil and the Good; and sendeth Rain on the Just and on the Unjust*[x]. And this Admonition is greatly strengthened, as each of us is directed to address himself to God, not as to his own Father merely, but as to *our Father,* the common Parent of Mankind. For there is inexpressible Force in that Argument, *Have we not all one Father? Hath not one God created us? Why do we deal treacherously,* or in any Respect unjustly or unkindly, *every man against his*

---

[n] Mal. i. 6.   [w] Luke xi. 13.   [x] Matth. v. 45.

Brother?

LECTURE XXX.

Brother [y]? And yet with greater Force still doth it hold to prevent mutual Injuries or Unkindnesses amongst Christians: who being, in a much closer and more endearing Sense, Children of God, and Brethren one to another, than the rest of the World; surely ought never to be, what they are too often, remarkably deficient in that reciprocal Affection, which was intended as the Token whereby *all Men should know them* [z].

Then, at the same Time, the Consideration, that this *our Father is in Heaven*, possessed of infinite Power and Glory, tends greatly to inspire us with Reverence towards him, at all Times, and in all Places, but in our Devotions peculiarly. And to this End it is pleaded by the wise King; *Keep thy Foot when thou goest to the House of God; be not rash with thy Mouth, and let not thine Heart be hasty to utter any Thing before God; for God is in Heaven, and thou upon Earth* [a]. It also tends no less to remind us, what the great End of our Prayers and our Lives should be: to obtain Admit-

[y] Mal. ii. 10.   [z] John xiii. 35.   [a] Eccl. v. 1, 2.

LECTURE XXX.

tance into that blessed Place, *where* God is, and *Christ sits on his right Hand*[b]. *For in his Presence is the Fulness of Joy; and at his right Hand, there is Pleasure for evermore*[c].

You see then, how many important Truths and Admonitions these few Words, which begin the Lord's Prayer, include: every Thing indeed, which can encourage us to pray, or dispose us to pray as we ought.

The Petition, which immediately follows, *Hallowed be thy Name*, is perhaps more liable to be repeated without being understood, than any of the rest: but when understood, as it easily may be, appears highly proper to stand in the very first Part of a Christian's Prayer. The Name of God means here God himself, his Person and Attributes: as it doth in many other Places of Scripture, where *fearing* or *blessing*, or *calling upon the Name of the Lord* is mentioned. And to *hallow his Name* signifies, to think of him as a Holy Being, and behave towards him accordingly. Now the Word, *Holy*, hath been already more

[b] Col. iii. 1.   [c] Psalm xvi. 12.

than

LECTURE XXX.

than once, in the Course of these Lectures, explained to mean whatever is worthy of being distinguished with serious Respect. And therefore all such Persons, Places, Things, and Times, as are set apart from vulgar Uses, and devoted to religious ones, are said in Scripture to be holy, and commanded to be hallowed. Now these being generally preserved with great Care, as they always ought, from whatever may defile and pollute them; hence the Term, *Holy*, came to signify what is clean and pure. And the most valuable Purity, beyond Comparison, being that of a Mind untainted by Sin, and secure from Tendencies towards it; Holiness more especially denotes this; and may in various Degrees be ascribed to Men and Angels; but in absolute Perfection to none, but God. For He, and He alone, is infinitely removed from all Possibility of doing, or thinking, or approving Evil.

This then is the Sense, in which we are to acknowledge, that *holy and reverend is his Name*[d]: this Conception of him is the Man-

[d] Psalm cxi. 9.

ner, in which we are to *hallow* it, and *sanctify the Lord God in our Hearts*[e]: a Matter of unspeakable Importance, and the very Foundation of all true Religion. For if we are not fully persuaded, that He is *of purer Eyes than to behold Evil*[f] with Indifference; if we imagine, that He can ever act unrighteously himself, or allow others to do so; that He is in any Case the Author of Sin; or esteems and loves any Thing in his Creatures, but Uprightness and Goodness; or shews himself to be other, than a perfectly great, and wise, and just, and gracious Being: so far as we do this, we mistake his Nature, and dishonour him; and set up an Idol of our own Fancy, instead of the true God. The Consequence of which will be, that in Proportion as our Notions of Him are false, our Worship, Imitation, and Obedience will be erroneous also; our Piety and our Morals will both be corrupted; we shall neglect what alone can recommend us to Him; we shall hope to please Him by Performances of no Value,

[e] 1 Pet. iii. 15. [f] Hab. i. 13.

Vol. II.　　　　L　　　　perhaps

perhaps by wicked Deeds; and *the Light, that is in us, will* become *Darkness* [g].

No Wonder then, if we are directed to make it our first Petition, that we and all Men may *hallow God's Name*, as we ought: that so right a Sense of his Nature and Attributes, especially his Wisdom, Justice, and Goodness, may prevail through the World, as may banish at once both Profaneness and Superstition, and engage us all to fear and love him equally: that we may entertain such Notions of Christianity, as will promote its Honour; and allow ourselves in nothing, that may bring Disgrace upon it, or tempt any to *blaspheme*, instead of sanctifying, *that worthy Name, by which we are called* [h]: but that each of us, in our Stations, may, with all Diligence, and all Prudence, propagate the Belief of *pure Religion and undefiled before God and the Father* [i]. This is the Way, and the only Way possible, for us truly to honour Him, and be truly good and happy: happy in ourselves, and in each other; in the present World, and that which is to come. With this Pe-

[g] Matth. vi. 23. [h] James ii. 7. [i] James i. 27.

tition therefore our bleſſed Lord moſt rationally directs us to begin. And let us all remember, that what He bids us pray for in the firſt Place, He will expect that we ſhould endeavour after in the firſt Place; and as we acknowledge *Him, who hath called us, to be holy,* that we ſhould *be holy* alſo *in all Manner of Converſation* [k].

[k] 1 Pet. i. 15.

LECTURE XXXI.

Thy Kingdom come, Thy Will be done.

THE second Petition of the Lord's Prayer, *Thy Kingdom come*, follows very naturally after the first, *Hallowed be thy Name*. For hallowing the Name of God, that is, entertaining just Notions, and being possessed with a deep Sense, of the Holiness of his Nature, his Abhorrence of Sin, his Justice and Goodness; is the necessary Preparative for submitting to, and being faithful Subjects of, that Kingdom, for the Coming of which we are directed to pray.

God indeed is, ever was, and cannot but be, Lord and King of the whole World, possessed of all Right and all Dominion, over all Things: as the plainest Reason shews, and the Conclusion of this very Prayer, in Conformity to the rest of Scripture, acknowledges. In this Senfe therefore we cannot pray for his Kingdom, as fomething future, but only rejoice in its being actually prefent: for what can be greater Joy, than to live under the Government of infinite Mercy, Wifdom, and Power? *The Lord reigneth: let the Earth rejoice, let the Multitude of Ifles be glad thereof* [a].

But befides this natural Kingdom of God, there is a moral and fpiritual one, founded on the willing Obedience of reafonable Creatures to thofe Laws of Righteoufnefs, which he hath given them. Now this, we have too plain Evidence, is not yet come amongft Men, fo fully as it ought. The very firft of human Race revolted from their Maker; and their Defcendants, as both Scripture and other Hiftory fhews, grew, Age after Age, yet more and more difobedient; till at length the Inhabitants of the whole Earth, inftead of being the happy Subjects of God's rightful Empire, became, by immoral Lives, and idolatrous Worfhip, moft wretched Slaves

[a] Pfalm xcvii. 1.

LECTURE XXXI.

to the ufurped Dominion of the wicked one. The Wifdom and Goodnefs of God made immediate Provifion, through his only Son our Lord, to oppofe this Kingdom of Darknefs, as foon as it appeared in the World: not by his abfolute Power; for Obedience lofes its Value, unlefs it proceed from Choice; but by the rational Method of Inftructions, Promifes, and Warnings from Heaven, fupcradded to what Nature taught, and fuited to the Circumftances of every Age.

These he gave at firft by the Patriarchs to all Men promifcuoufly: and whoever acknowledged his Authority, and obeyed his Laws, was a good Subject and true Member of his Kingdom. But when afterwards, notwithftanding this Care, the Corruption of Mankind was become general, He chofe the Pofterity of his Servant *Abraham*, and diftinguifhed them by his efpecial Favour: not as cafting off the reft of the World; for *in every Nation, at all Times, they that fear God, and work Righteoufnefs, are accepted with him* [b]: but that, in this

---
[b] Acts x. 35.

LECTURE XXXI.

People at least, the Profession of Faith in Him, and subjection to Him, might be kept alive; not merely for their own Benefit, but the Information of others also. With them therefore was the Kingdom of God, in a peculiar Degree, for 1500 Years. While they flourished in their own Land, they held forth the Light of Truth to all the Nations round them. And when they were led captive or dispersed into other Lands, they spread it yet farther: and thus were great Instruments in preparing the rest of Mankind for that general Re-establishment of Obedience to the true God, as King and Lord of all, which our blessed Saviour came to effect.

The Gospel Dispensation therefore having this for its End, and being much more perfectly fitted to attain it, than any preceding Manifestation of Religion had been; the Scripture, in a distinguished Manner, calls it *the Kingdom of God*, or *of Heaven:* both which Words denote, in exactly the same View, that Dominion, which in *Daniel* it is foretold *the God of Heaven should set up, and which should never be destroyed.*

LECTURE XXXI.

deſtroyed[c]. Our Saviour was then, after *John* the Baptiſt, only giving Notice of its Approach, and opening the Way for ſetting it up, when he firſt directed his Diſciples to pray, that it might come. By his Death He raiſed it on the Ruins of the Devil's Uſurpation, *over whom He triumphed on his Croſs*[d]: and now it hath been many Ages in the World. But ſtill it is by no Means come, in that Extent, and to that good Effect, which we have Reaſon to beg that it may, and to believe that it will. The largeſt Part of Mankind hath not, ſo much as in Profeſſion, entered into this Kingdom: but lies overwhelmed in Pagan Idolatry, Jewiſh Unbelief, or Mahometan Deluſion. The largeſt Part of Chriſtians have corrupted the Doctrine of Chriſt with grievous Errors: and thoſe who preſerve the pureſt Faith, too generally live ſuch impure and wicked Lives; that, though the Kingdom of God hath indeed taken Place amongſt them in outward Appearance, yet in that Senſe, which will prove at laſt the only important one,

[c] Dan. ii. 44. [d] Col. ii. 15.

they

they are still far from it. *For the Kingdom of God*, saith our Saviour, *is within you* [e]: and consists, as the Apostle further explains it, *in Righteousness and Peace, and Joy in the* Graces of the *Holy Ghost* [f].

Here then is great Room, and great Need, for praying; that the *Heathen* may become *the Inheritance of* Christ, *and the uttermost Parts of the* Mahometan *World his Possession* [g]: that the Jews, *from whom*, for their Unbelief, *the Kingdom of God hath been* so long *taken* [h] away, may be restored to a Share in it; as the Prophets, both of the Old and New Testament, have foretold they shall: and lastly, *that all who profess and call themselves Christians, may* not only *be led into the Way of Truth*, but *hold the Faith in Unity of Spirit, in the Bond of Peace, and in Righteousness of Life* [i]. How little Prospect soever there may be at present of such Happiness as this, yet *we have a sure Word of Prophecy* [k]:, for the Ground of our Prayers, that the Time shall come, when *the Kingdoms of this World shall be the*

[e] Luke xvii. 21. [f] Rom. xiv. 17. [g] Psalm ii. 8.
[h] Matth. xxi. 43. [i] Prayer for all Conditions of Men.
[k] 2 Pet. i. 19.

Kingdoms

LECTURE XXXI.

Kingdoms of our God and of his Christ[l], in a Degree that they have never been yet: when *all the People shall be righteous* [m], and *know the Lord, from the greatest unto the least* [n].

But the Kingdom of God upon Earth, even in its best Estate, is comparatively but short-lived and imperfect, indeed a mere Introduction to that glorious and eternal Manifestation of it in Heaven, which ought ever to be the Object of our most ardent Desires and Requests. For as the Governor, and the Governed, and the great fundamental Laws of Government, are still to be the same, in the present State of Trial, and the future one of Recompence; they both make up together but one Kingdom of God. And therefore, when we pray for the coming of it, we pray in the last Place, for the Arrival of that Time, when the King and Judge of all *shall sit upon the Throne of his Glory* [o], and *reward every Man according to his Works* [p]; when *the Righteous shall shine forth, as the Sun, in the Kingdom of their*

[l] Rev. xi. 15. [m] Isa. lx. 21. [n] Jer. xxxi. 34.
[o] Matth. xxv. 31. [p] Matth. xvi. 27.

Father;

Father q; even that *Kingdom which was prepared for them from the Foundation of the World* r; and *shall reign with Him* in it *for ever and ever* s.

But then, as we pray for this Time, we must prepare for it also; else we do nothing but ask our own Condemnation; as the Prophet *Amos* hath most awfully warned us: *Wo unto you that desire the Day of the Lord. To what End is it for you? The Day of the Lord is Darkness, and not Light* t.

To instruct us therefore, on what it is, that our Share in the Kingdom of God depends, our Saviour immediately subjoins another Petition, expressing it very clearly: *Thy Will be done in Earth as it is in Heaven.* For *not every one that saith unto Him, Lord, Lord, shall enter into the Kingdom of Heaven* u: but they only who *do the Will of God, shall receive his Promise* w.

Indeed what God *wills* to do Himself, that *He doth accordingly,* both *in the Army of Heaven, and amongst the Inhabitants of the Earth; and none can stay his Hand* x. But

q Matth. xiii. 43.   r Matth. xxv. 34.   s Rev. xx. 6. xxii. 5.   t Amos v. 18.   u Matth. vii. 21. w Heb. x. 36.   x Dan. iv. 35.

what

LECTURE XXXI.

what He wills Us to do, that He only requires of us, as we value his Favour, or fear his Displeasure; leaving us designedly that Power of not doing what he bids us, without which, doing it were no Virtue. But though Disobedience to his Will is in our Power; yet Obedience is not so, without the Assistance of his Grace: which therefore, in these Words, we desire for ourselves, and for all Men. And since, by the Means of Prayer, we may have Strength to obey his Will granted us; we are certainly, with as much Justice, expected to obey it, as if we had the Power already of our own.

Now the Will of God consists in these two Things: That we suffer patiently what He lays upon us, and perform faithfully what he commands us. The former of these; to bear with Resignation whatever, in any Kind, God sees proper to inflict; and, though we may wish and pray for the Prevention or Removal of Sufferings, yet to be content, nay desirous, that *his Will* should *be done, not ours* [y] ; may often prove a

[y] Luke xxii. 42.

difficult,

difficult, but is always an evident and neceſſary, Duty. For to indulge a contrary Diſpoſition, is to ſet up ourſelves above our Maker; to rebel againſt his Authority, deny his Wiſdom, and diſtruſt his Goodneſs. The Ability therefore of ſubmitting meekly to his Pleaſure, is undoubtedly one great Thing that we are to requeſt, and endeavour to obtain.

But ſtill, as the bleſſed Inhabitants of Heaven ſurely have little or no Occaſion for this Kind of Obedience, we have Reaſon to think that the other, the active Sort, is the Point which our Saviour deſigned we ſhould principally have in View, when we beg, that God's Will may be done by us, as it is by them: by *his Angels, that fulfil his Commandments, hearkening unto the Voice of his Words; thoſe Miniſters of his, that do his Pleaſure*[z]. Not that we can hope to equal the Services of Beings placed ſo much above us: but only inſpire to ſuch Reſemblance of them, that our Obedience may bear the ſame Proportion to our Abilities, which that of the heavenly Spirits doth to theirs.

[z] Pſ. ciii. 20, 21.

LECTURE XXXI.

Their Knowledge of God's Will is clear and diſtinct: on which Account, the higheſt Character given of human Wiſdom is, to be *as an Angel of God, to diſcern Good and Bad* [a]. It ſhould therefore, when we make Uſe of this Petition, be our Deſire that We alſo, in our Degree, may *be not unwiſe, but underſtanding what the Will of the Lord is* [b], and *may abound, more and more, in Knowledge and in all Judgment* [c]. They do every Thing, without Exception, which they know to be God's Pleaſure: whereas we are very apt to omit Part, and perform the reſt but imperfectly. They do it with Alacrity and Chearfulneſs: whereas we too often ſhew great Backwardneſs and Reluctance. They do it alſo from a real Principle of Duty: whereas, were the Truth but known, as to God it is known, a great Share of the good Actions, upon which we value ourſelves, are perhaps only good Appearances; proceeding, ſome from Conſtitution, ſome from worldly Prudence, ſome from Vanity; few, it may be doubted, principally, and fewer yet, entirely from the Love

[a] 2 Sam. xiv. 17. [b] Eph. v. 17. [c] Phil. i. 9.

or Fear of God, from Esteem of Virtue, or Hatred of Sin. In these Respects then we must earnestly pray, and diligently endeavour, to be like the holy Angels: and were we but like them in one Thing more; that they all, without Exception, do the Will of God, and have none amongst them disobedient to it; then would our Earth resemble Heaven indeed. How far this is from being the Case, we know too well. But notwithstanding let us comfort ourselves with considering, that as the Time was when even these blessed Spirits had a Mixture of evil ones amongst them; so the Time will be, when we shall have no such Mixture amongst us: but shall become, in this and all Respects, *as the Angels of God in Heaven*[d].

[d] Matth. xxii. 30.

LECTURE XXXII.

Give us this Day our daily Bread: And forgive us our Trespasses, as we forgive them that trespass against us.

THE three former of the six Petitions of the Lord's Prayer express our earnest Desires, that we, and all our Fellow-Creatures, may attain the great End of our Creation, that is, may understand, receive, and practise, true Religion, to God's Honour and our own eternal Happiness: after which we proceed, in the three last, to ask of Him the Means to this End; such Supplies of our Wants, as will be needful for the Performance of our Duties. And they are comprehended under three Heads more: the Relief of our temporal Necessities, the Forgiveness of our past Sins, and the Assistance of his Grace against future Temptations.

LECTURE XXXII.

The first of these Blessings we request, by saying, *Give us this Day our daily Bread.* All the good Things of Life, and all our Capacity of receiving Support and Comfort from them, proceed, as every Thing doth, from God's free Gift; and therefore depend, as every Thing doth, on his free Pleasure: for what He hath bestowed, He can, with just the same Ease, at any Time, take away. He hath placed Things indeed in a regular, and what we call a natural, Course and Order. But this Order is not only of his own appointing, but his own preserving too. *He* it is, that *maketh his Sun to rise*[a]; that *giveth us Rain from Heaven, and fruitful Seasons, filling our Hearts with Food and Gladness*[b]. Were He only thus kind to us all in general, it would certainly be our Duty to acknowledge his Kindness, and pray for the Continuance of it. But as we learn from Scripture further, that his Providence extends, even in the minutest Instances, to each of us in particular; and that not the smallest Thing comes to pass, but by his Appointment, or

[a] Matt. v. 45. [b] Acts xvi. 17.

LECTURE XXXII.

wife Permiffion^c; this furnifhes additional Reafons for applying to Him, that his continual Superintendency may be ever exercifed towards us for our Good. We know not indeed with Certainty, in thefe Matters, what will be good for us. But ftill, fince He hath given us Defires, infeparable from our Frame, of enjoying Life to its ordinary Term, with a competent Share of the feveral Accommodations which contribute to make it agreeable; it muft be lawful to exprefs thofe Defires to Him in a proper Manner. And this our Saviour directs us how to do, when He bids us petition for *our daily Bread*.

The Word *Bread*, as it frequently fignifies in Scripture all Sorts of Food, fo it may very naturally fignify, what it doth in this Prayer, all Sorts of Things requifite in human Life. This *Agur* meant, when he prayed, that God would *feed him with Food* (in the original it is *Bread*) *convenient for him*^d. And this we mean in common Difcourfe, as often as we fpeak of Perfons getting their *Bread*. But then it muft by

^c Matth. x. 29, 30. Luke xii. 6, 7.   ^d Prov. xxx. 8.

no Means be extended beyond Things requisite; those, without which we are unable either to subsist at all, or however conveniently and comfortably. Not that Desires of further Advantages in the World are universally unlawful. But they are so apt to enlarge, and swell into extravagant and sinful Passions; into Schemes of Luxury, or Vanity, or Covetousness; that we have usually much more Need to restrain and check, than authorize them, by asking the Accomplishment of them from God; lest we be guilty of what St. *James* condemns, *asking amiss, that we may consume it upon our Lusts* [e].

It is therefore only for such a Share of worldly Good, as to a reasonable and moderate Mind will appear sufficient, that our Saviour allows us here to pray; in the Spirit which *Agur*, in the Prayer just mentioned, expresses; *Give me neither Poverty nor Riches: feed me with Food convenient for me. Lest I be full and deny Thee, and say, Who is the Lord? or lest I be poor and steal, and take the Name of God in vain* [f]. For

[e] Jam. iv. 13.   [f] Prov. xxx. 8, 9.

indeed,

LECTURE XXXII.

indeed, though the Temptations of extreme Poverty are very great; yet the Tendency of Wealth and Eafe and Power, to Senfuality and Pride and Forgetfulnefs of God, is fo exceeding ftrong, that a well-inftructed and confiderate Mind would rather fubmit, than chufe to be placed in a Condition of Abundance and Eminence. For preferving the Order, and conducting the Affairs of the World, fome muft be in fuch Stations: but let all who are, look well to their Ways; and let none of their Inferiors envy them.

It ought to be further obferved here, that our bleffed Lord hath not only confined us to pray for *our Bread*, but *our daily Bread*; to be given us, as we afk for it, Day by Day: intending, doubtlefs, to make us remember and acknowledge, that our Dependance on God is continual, from one Moment to another: that they, who have the moft of this World, have it only during his Pleafure; and are bound, both to afk, and receive, every Day's Enjoyment of it, as a new Gift from Him: while at the fame Time, they who have leaft may be affured, that what He hath commanded them to pray for, He will ordinarily not fail to bestow upon them; by blessing their Endeavours, if they are able to use Endeavours; or by stirring up the Charity of others towards them, if they are not.

For as to those who can labour, Industry is the Method by which God hath thought fit to give them their Bread; and therefore, by which they ought to seek it. They have no Title to it any other Way; St. *Paul* having directed, *that, if any one will not work, neither should he eat* [g]. Nor must they work only to supply their present Necessities: but, by Diligence and Frugality, lay up something, if possible, for future Exigencies also: learning of *the Ant, which provideth her Meat in the Summer, and gathereth her Food in the Harvest* [h].

So that applying for our daily Bread to God, is far from excluding a proper Care to use the appointed Means of procuring it for ourselves. But if our Care be a presumptuous one, and void of Regard to the Disposer of all Things; we provoke Him

[g] 2 Thess. iii. 10.   [h] Prov. vi. 8.

LECTURE XXXII.

to blast our fairest Hopes. And if it be an anxious and distrustful one, we think injuriously of Him to whom we pray: who can as easily give us the Bread of Tomorrow, as He gave us that of Yesterday. Nay, if our worldly Cares, though they do not disquiet our Minds, yet engross them; if we carry our Attention to this World so far as to forget the next; or imagine ourselves to be securer in Stores *laid up for many years*[i], than in God's good Providence: this also is very unsuitable to the Spirit, both of our Lord's Prayer, and of his whole Religion; which commands us to *seek first the Kingdom of God and his Righteousness*[k], and *not to trust in uncertain Riches, but in Him, who giveth us richly all Things to enjoy*[l].

I shall only add two Observations more, which have been made very justly on this Petition[m]: that, since we ask our Bread from God, we ought not to accept it from the Devil; that is, to gain our Subsistence by any unlawful Means: and that, since we

---

[i] Luke xii. 19.   [k] Matth. vi. 33.   [l] 1 Tim. vi. 17.
[m] By Bp. Blackhall.

do not say, *Give me my daily Bread*; but, *Give us ours*; we entreat God to supply the Wants of others, as well as our own. Now the Means, which He hath provided for supplying the Wants of the helpless Poor, is the Charity of the Rich. And to pray Him, that they may be relieved, and yet withhold from them what He hath designed for their Relief, is just that Piece of Inconsistence or Hypocrisy, which St. *James* so strongly exposes. *If a Brother, or Sister, be naked, and destitute of daily Food; and one of you say unto them, Depart in Peace, be ye warmed, and be ye filled ; notwithstanding ye give them not those Things which are needful to the Body : what doth it profit*[n]?

From our temporal Wants, we proceed next to a much more important Concern, our spiritual ones: and here we ask in the first Place, what it is very fit we should, Pardon and Mercy. *Forgive us our Trespasses, as we forgive them that trespass against us.* The Forgiveness of Sins having been already explained, under that Article of the Creed, which relates to it; I shall only

[n] James ii. 15. 16.

take

LECTURE XXXII.

take Notice at prefent of the Argument, which we are directed to ufe in pleading for it, which is likewife the efpecial Condition of our obtaining it; that *we alfo forgive*º, as we hope to be forgiven. And concerning this, two Things ought to be underftood: what that Forgivenefs is, to which we are bound; and how far the Exercife of it will avail us.

Now the Obligation to Forgivenefs means, not that the Magiftrate is to omit punifhing Malefactors; *for he is the Minifter of God, a Revenger, to execute* Wrath upon him, *that doth Evil*ᴾ: not that the Rulers of the Church are to forbear fpiritual Cenfures againft notorious Offenders; for the Scripture hath appointed them, for the Amendment of Sinners, and the Prefervation of the Innocent, when they are likely to have thefe good Effects: not that private Perfons do amifs in bringing Tranfgreffors to Juftice; for neglecting it would be in general only a feeming Kindnefs to them, and a real Mifchief to human Society: not that we are forbidden to make

º Luke xi. 4.   ᴾ Rom. xiii. 4.

reafonable

sonable Demands on such, as withhold our Dues, or do us any Damage: for recovering a Debt is a very different Thing from revenging an Injury: nor lastly, that we are always bound, when Persons have behaved ill to us, either to think as well of them as before; which may be impossible; or to trust and favour them as much; which may be unwise. But our Obligation to forgive doth mean, and absolutely require, that, civil Governors be moderate and merciful; and ecclesiastical ones, make use of Discipline *to Edification, not to Destruction*[q]: that, in our private Capacity, we pass by all Offences, which, with Safety, to ourselves, and the Public, we can: that where we must punish, we do it with Reluctance; and as gently, as the Case will permit; and where we must defend or recover our Rights, we do it with the least Expence, and the least Uneasiness to the adverse Party, that may be: that we never be guilty of Injustice to others, because they have been guilty of it to us; and never refuse them proper Favours, merely because we have been refused

[q] 2 Cor. x. 8. xiii. 10.

such

LECTURE XXXII.

such Favours by them; much less, because we have not obtained from them what it was not fit we should: that we look upon little Provocations, as Trifles: and be careful, not to think great ones greater than they are: that we be willing to make those who have displeased us, all such Allowances to the full, as our common Frailty and Ignorance demand: that we always wish well to them; and be ready, as soon as ever we have real Cause, to think well of them; to believe their Repentance; and, how great or many soever their Faults may have been, to accept it; and restore them to as large a Share of our Kindness and Friendship, as any wise and good Person, uninterested in the Question, would think safe and right: always remembering, in every Case of Injury, how very apt we are to err on the severe Side; and how very much better it is, to err on the merciful one.

This is the Temper of Forgiveness to our Fellow-Creatures: and it is plainly a good and fit Temper. Let us therefore now consider further, what Influence it will have

have towards our Maker's forgiving us. Our Saviour undoubtedly lays a peculiar Stress on it for this Purpose; both by inserting it, as a Condition, into the Body of his Prayer; and insisting on it, as a necessary one, in his Words immediately after the Prayer. But still, we must observe, He doth not mention it as the Cause, that procures our Forgiveness: for *God saveth us, not by* this, or any other *Works of Righteousness, which we do, but according to his Mercy; which He hath shed on us abundantly through Jesus Christ; that being justified by his Grace, we may be Heirs of eternal Life* [r]. Our pardoning others is no more than a Qualification, requisite to our receiving that final Pardon from God, which our Saviour, through the Divine Goodness, hath merited by his Death, on that Condition. Nor is it the only Qualification necessary, though it be a principal one. For the rest of God's Laws were given in vain, if observing this one would secure his Favour: and *Christ* would be found *the Minister of Sin* [s], if He had taught, that the single good Disposition of

[r] Tit. iii. 5, 6, 7.   [s] Gal. ii. 17.

Forgiveness

LECTURE XXXII.

Forgiveness would be sufficient, let a Person have ever so many bad ones. But it is plain, that throughout the whole Sermon on the Mount, in which this Prayer is delivered, He makes the Performance of every Part of our Duty, the Condition of our Acceptance. In the very Beginning of it, He hath promised Heaven to several other Virtues, as well as here to this; and the Meaning is, not that Persons may get thither by any one, that they will; for nobody sure is so bad, as to have none at all: but that each of them shall have its proper Share, in fitting us for that Mercy and Reward, which however, with less than all of them, we shall never obtain. Our Imperfections in all will indeed be pardoned: but not our Continuance in a wilful Neglect of any.

Still, though a Spirit of Forgiveness to our Brother is by no Means the Whole, that God requires in order to forgive Us; yet it is a Quality, often so difficult, always so important, and so peculiarly needful to be exercised by us, when we are intreating our Maker to exercise it towards us; that our Saviour had great Reason to place it in the

strong

strong Light, which he hath done; and even to place it single; since his Design could not easily be understood to be any other, than to engage our particular Attention to what deserves it so much. For if we will not, for the Love of God, and in Obedience to his Command, pardon our Fellow-Creatures the few and small Injuries, which they are able to do us; (when perhaps we may have done many Things to provoke them, and comparatively can have done little to oblige or serve them) how should we ever expect, that He will forgive us the numerous and heinous Offences, which we have committed against Him: from whom we have received all that we have, on whom we depend for all that we can hope for, to whom therefore we owe the most unreserved Duty, and the most affectionate Gratitude?

Let us remember then, that since we pray to be forgiven, only as we forgive; so often as we use these Words, we pray in Effect for God's Vengeance upon ourselves, instead of his Mercy, if we forgive not. And therefore, let us apply to Him continually

LECTURE XXXII.

continually for Grace to do in earneſt, what we profeſs to do in this Petition: let us carefully examine our Hearts and our Conduct, that we may not cheat ourſelves, for we cannot cheat God, with falſe Pretences of obſerving this Duty, while indeed we tranſgreſs it; let us utterly *put away from us, all Bitterneſs, and Wrath, and Clamour, and Evil-ſpeaking, with all Malice; and be kind one to another, tender-hearted, forgiving one another;* even as we hope, that God, *for Chriſt's Sake, will forgive us* [t].

[t] Eph. iv. 31, 32.

LECTURE XXXIII.

And lead us not into Temptation; but deliver us from Evil: for thine is the Kingdom, and the Power, and the Glory, for ever and ever. Amen.

WE should be very unfit to ask for the Pardon of our past Sins; and could neither hope to obtain it, nor indeed continue long the better for it; if we did not earnestly desire, at the same Time, to avoid Sin for the future. And therefore, after the Petition, *Forgive us our Trespasses,* most properly follows, *and lead us not into Temptation.*

The Word *Temptation* very often signifies no more, than Trial; any Opposition or Difficulty, that may call forth our Virtues into vigorous Practice, and, by so doing, both strengthen and make them known: not indeed to God, who always knows our Hearts; but to ourselves and others,

LECTURE XXXIII.

to those around us at present; to all Mankind, and the holy Angels hereafter. Now in this general Sense, our whole Life on Earth is, and was intended to be, a State of Temptation: in which, as the Scripture expresses it, *God* himself *tempts* Men [a]; that is, proves and exercises them. And accordingly, St. *James* directs us to *count it all Joy when we fall into divers Temptations*; adding a very good Reason for it: *Blessed is the the Man, that endureth Temptation: for when he is tried, he shall receive the Crown of Life; which the Lord hath promised to them, that love Him* [b]. The more Love to God we thus shew; the more we exert our inward good Principles and Habits, and by exerting, improve them: the greater Reward we shall obtain. When therefore we say, *Lead us not into Temptation*; we do not pray, that we may not be tried at all: for we know, that we must, even for our own Good.

But the Word here stands for dangerous Trials, Provocations, and Enticements to Sin: under which we are likely to sink,

[a] Gen. xxii. 1.   Deut. iv. 34.   2 Chron. xxxii. 31.
[b] James i. 2, 12.

instead

LECTURE XXXIII.

inſtead of overcoming them. Now there is indeed ſcarce any Thing in Life, that may not be a Temptation to us, in this bad Senſe. Our Tempers, our Ages, our Stations, and Employments in the World, be they ever ſo different, may, each in their different Ways, riſk our Innocence. They that are poor, are grievouſly tempted, either to repine againſt God; or take unlawful Methods of relieving themſelves. And *they that will be Rich*, Experience, as well as the Apoſtle, may teach us, *fall into Temptation and a Snare, and into many fooliſh and hurtful Luſts*[c]. Both Adverſity and Proſperity, Buſineſs and Leiſure, Company and Solitude, have their reſpective Hazards. And ſometimes theſe Hazards are ſo dreadfully heightened by particular Circumſtances; and, at others, trying Incidents, totally unforeſeen, happen ſo unſeaſonably; that, though they may only rouſe and animate our Virtue; yet they may alſo, more probably, overbear, and deſtroy it. And therefore we muſt know very little of our natural Frailty, the Strength of our Paſſions,

[c] 1 Tim. vi. 9.

and *the Deceitfulness of Sin* [d]; if we do not think it the more prudent, as well as modester, Part, to decline, than venture the Conflict, if it be God's Will: and do not accordingly beg of Him, that He would *not lead us into* such *Temptation*.

God, indeed, *tempts no Man* [e], in the Sense of alluring and inviting him to Sin; as the Devil, and wicked People, and our own bad Hearts do. And therefore to pray, in this Sense, that He would *not lead us into Temptation*, would be great Irreverence, instead of Piety: for it is inconsistent with the Holiness of his Nature, that He should. But as nothing comes to pass, but with his Knowledge and Sufferance; and every Thing is subject to his Direction and Superintendency: the Scripture speaks, as if every Thing was done by Him, when the Meaning, as appears by other Passages of it, is only to acknowledge, that nothing is done without Him: and, agreeably to the Manner of Speaking in the Eastern Countries, Things are ascribed to Him, which He only permits, and afterwards turns to the

[d] Heb. iii. 13.   [e] James i. 13.

LECTURE XXXIII.

Furtherance of his own good Purposes. Now God may very justly permit us to be led into the severest Temptations, if we do not pray to Him against it: because a great Part of the Danger proceeds from that Weakness, which we have wilfully, or carelessly brought upon ourselves; and Prayer is one of the Means, that He hath appointed for our Preservation and Relief; which Means, if we use as we ought, He *will not suffer us to be tempted above that we are able; but will, with the Temptation, also make a Way to escape, that we may be able to bear it* [f].

But if, through Pride or Negligence, we will not ask for his Help, we must not expect it. And though we do for Form's Sake ask it, if we have little Faith in it, or Dependence on it, St. *James* hath foretold the Event: *Let not that Man think, that he shall receive any Thing of the Lord* [g]. Yet, on the other Hand, if we carry our Dependence so far, as presumptuously to run into those Dangers, out of which we beg Him to keep us; or, at least, will do

[f] 1 Cor. x. 13.   [g] James i. 7.

little

little or nothing to keep ourselves out of them, instead of doing every Thing that we can; or if, in the Dangers, in which He may think fit to place us, we will not use our best Endeavours to stand, as well as pray that we may not fall; such Prayers can never be likely to avail for our Protection. But fervent Devotion, hearty Resolution, and prudent Care, united and continued, will do any Thing. By whatever Difficulties we are surrounded, and how little Possibility soever we may see of getting through them; still, *Commit thy Way unto the Lord, put thy Trust in Him, and He shall bring it to pass* [h].

In the second Part of this Petition, *But deliver us from Evil*; the Word *Evil* may signify, either Sin and its Consequences; or the great Tempter to Sin, the *evil* or *wicked One*; for by that Name the Devil is often called in the New Testament [i]. The Number indeed of wicked Spirits is probably very great: but notwithstanding this, being united, under one Head, in one De-

[h] Psalm xxxvii. 5.   [i] Matth. xiii. 19, 38.   1 John ii. 13, 14. iii. 12. v. 18.

LECTURE XXXIII.

sign of obstructing our Salvation, they are all comprehended under one Name. And since, in our present State of Trial, we have *not* only, as Experience shews, *Flesh and Blood to wrestle against*; our own bad Disposition, and the Solicitations of a bad World, to resist; but also, as the Word of God informs us, *Principalities and Powers, and spiritual Wickedness in high Places* [k], an Army of invisible Enemies, employing to overcome us, and not less formidably because imperceptibly, all the Stratagems, that Heaven allows them to use; this, as it increases our Danger, may well quicken our Prayers for Safety and Deliverance. That there should be evil Angels, as well as evil Men, of the greatest Abilities and Accomplishments, is, if rightly considered, no great Wonder: and that both should entice us to Sin, is no reasonable Discouragement: for let us but apply to God, and we shall not be left in the Power of either. What the Power of wicked Spirits is, we are not told in Scripture: and it is no Part of Religion, in the least, to believe idle Stories

[k] Eph. vi. 11, 12.

LECTURE XXXIII.

about them. Of this we are sure, that they have no Power, but what God permits: and He will never permit them to do, what shall prove, in the End, any Hurt to those, who serve and fear Him. More especially we are sure, that they cannot in the least, either force us into sinning, or hinder us from repenting. Invite or dissuade us they may, by suggesting false Notions of the Pleasure, or Profit, or Harmlessness of Sin: by representing God, as too good to be angry, or too severe to be reconciled: by describing to our Imaginations, Repentance to be so easy at any Time, that it is needless now; or so difficult now, that it is too late and impossible: by putting it into our Thoughts, that we are so good, we may be confident and careless; or so wicked, we must absolutely despair. It concerns us therefore greatly, *not to be ignorant of their Devices*[1]. But, provided we keep on our Guard; earnestly apply to God, and are true to ourselves; neither their Temptations, nor those of the whole World, shall prevail against us. For then only, as St.

[1] 2 Cor. ii. 11.

James

LECTURE XXXIII.

James gives us to underſtand, *is every Man tempted dangerouſly, when he is drawn away of his own Luſt, and enticed* [m]. The Enemy within, therefore, is the moſt formidable one: and againſt this it is chiefly, that we are to *watch, and pray, that we enter not into Temptation :* remembering always, that how *willing* ſoever *the Spirit* may be, yet *the Fleſh is weak* [n].

And now let us obſerve, in the laſt Place, under this Head, that as we are to pray againſt being led into Temptation ourſelves, we ſhould be very careful, never to lead others into it; but do every Thing that we can, to keep them out of it, and deliver them from it: and that, as begging God's Help that we may ſtand, muſt be grounded on a ſtrong Senſe of our Proneneſs to fall; we ſhould ſhew great Compaſſion towards them, who, through the ſame Proneneſs, have fallen. *Brethren, if a Man be overtaken in a Fault; ye, which are ſpiritual, reſtore ſuch a one in the Spirit of Meekneſs: conſidering thyſelf, leſt thou alſo be tempted* [o].

[m] James i. 14.   [n] Matth. xxvi. 41.   [o] Gal. vi. 1.

Thus

LECTURE XXXIII.

Thus we have gone through the six Petitions, which compose the second Part of the Lord's Prayer; and shew it to be worthy of its Author, by distinctly comprehending, in so little Room, whatever is necessary for the Honour of God, and our own Good, both temporal and spiritual. What remains further is, to speak briefly of the third Part, which concludes the Whole, by ascribing to our heavenly Father, the Praise *due unto his Name* [p] *:* acknowledging here more expresly, what indeed hath been throughout implied, that His *is the Kingdom*, the rightful Authority and supreme Dominion over all: His *the Power*, by which every Thing just and good is brought to pass; His therefore *the Glory* of whatever we his Creatures do, or enjoy, or hope for; of whatever this Universe, and the whole Scheme of Things which it comprehends, hath had, or now hath, or ever shall have in it, awful or gracious, and worthy of the Admiration of Men and Angels. And as all Dignity and Might and Honour are His; so they are His *for*

[p] Psalm xxix. 2.

LECTURE XXXIII.

ever and ever: originally, independently and unchangeably. *From everlasting to everlasting He is God*[q]*: the same Yesterday, To-day, and for ever*[r].

These Words then are, at once, an Act of Homage to his Greatness, and Thanksgiving to his Goodness: both which ought ever to have a Place in our Prayers; and the Conclusion is a very proper Place. For the infinite Perfections of God our Maker, which we thus celebrate, are the best Reason possible for every Petition that we have offered to Him: and therefore our blessed Lord introduces them as the Reason. *For thine is the Kingdom, and the Power, and the Glory.* Besides, ending with these Acknowledgments will leave them fresh and strong upon our Minds: especially as we finish all with that solemn Asseveration, *Amen*: which is a Word, used in Scripture, only upon serious and important Occasions, to confirm the Truth and Sincerity of what is promised, wished, or affirmed. It relates therefore equally to the Whole of the Prayer: and is in Effect declaring, that

[q] Pf. xc. 2.   [r] Heb. xiii. 8.

we do heartily believe whatever we have said, and heartily desire whatever we have asked.

This Expression therefore may remind us, that our Prayers should always be composed, both in such a Language, and such Words in that Language, as all, that are to use or join in them, are well acquainted with. For else, as St. *Paul* argues, *How shall he, that occupieth the Room of the Unlearned, say, Amen: seeing he understandeth not what thou sayest* [s]?

And it should likewise remind us very strongly of another Thing, if possible, yet more important: that we should never say to God, what we cannot say with the utmost truth of Heart. Now with what Truth, or what Face, can any Person, that lives in any Sin, repeat the Prayer which our Lord hath taught us, and say *Amen* to it; when every Sentence in it, if well considered, is inconsistent with a bad Life? Let us therefore consider both it and ourselves very carefully, that we may offer up our Devotions always in an acceptable

[s] 1 Cor. xiv. 16.

Manner.

LECTURE XXXIII.

Manner. For *the Sacrifice of the Wicked is an Abomination to the Lord : but the Prayer of the Upright is his Delight* [t].

[t] Prov. xv. 8.

LECTURE XXXIV.

The Nature and Number of the Sacraments.

THE far greatest Part of the Duties which we owe to God, flow, as it were, of themselves, from his Nature and Attributes, and the several Relations to Him, in which we stand, whether made known to us by Reason or Scripture. Such are those, which have been hitherto explained to you: the ten Commandments; and Prayer for the Grace, which our fallen Condition requires, in order to keep them. But there are still some other important Precepts peculiar to Christianity, and deriving their whole Obligation from our Saviour's Institution of them: concerning which it is highly requisite that our Catechism should instruct us, before it concludes. And these are the two Sacraments.

The

LECTURE XXXIV.

The Word *Sacrament*, by Virtue of its Original in the Latin Tongue, signifies any sacred or holy Thing or Action: and among the Heathens was particularly applied to denote sometimes a Pledge, deposited in a sacred Place[a]; sometimes an Oath, the most sacred of Obligations; and especially that Oath of Fidelity, which the Soldiery took to their General. In Scripture it is not used at all. By the early Writers of the Western Church, it was used to express almost any Thing relating to our holy Religion; at least any Thing that was figurative, and signified somewhat further than at first Sight appeared. But afterwards, a more confined Use of the Word prevailed by Degrees: and in that stricter Sense, which hath long been the common one, and which our Catechism follows, the Nature of a Sacrament comprehends the following Particulars:

1. There must be *an outward and visible Sign*: the solemn Application of some bodily and sensible Thing or Action, to a Meaning and Purpose which in its own Na-

[a] Eden. Elem. Jur. Civ. p. 238. Gronov. in Plaut. Rud. 5. 3, 21.

ture

LECTURE XXXIV.

ture it hath not. In common Life, we have many other Signs to exprefs our Meanings, on Occafions of great Confequence, befides Words. And no Wonder then, if, in Religion, we have fome of the fame Kind.

2. In a Sacrament, the outward and vifible Sign muft denote *an inward and fpiritual Grace given unto us:* that is, fome Favour freely beftowed on us from Heaven; by which our inward and fpiritual Condition, the State of our Souls, is made better. Moft of the fignificative Actions, that we ufe in Religion, exprefs only our Duty to God. Thus kneeling in Prayer is ufed to fhew our Reverence towards Him to whom we pray. And figning a Child with the Crofs, after it is baptized, declares our Obligation not to be afhamed of the Crofs of Chrift. But a Sacrament, befides expreffing, on our Part, Duty to God, expreffes, on his Part, fome Grace or Favour towards us.

3. In order to intitle any Thing to the Name of a Sacrament, a further Requifite is, that it be *ordained by Chrift himfelf*. We may indeed ufe, on the foot of human Authority alone, Actions, that fet forth either

LECTURE XXXIV.

our fenfe of any Duty, or our Belief in God's Grace. For it is certainly as lawful to exprefs a good Meaning by any other proper Sign as by Words. But then, fuch Marks as thefe, which we commonly call Ceremonies, as they are taken up at Pleafure, may be laid afide again at Pleafure; and ought to be laid afide, whenever they grow too numerous, or Abufes are made of them, which cannot eafily be reformed; and this hath frequently been the Cafe. But Sacraments are of perpetual Obligation; for they ftand on the Authority of Chrift; who hath certainly appointed nothing to be for ever obferved in his Church, but what He faw would be for ever ufeful. Nor doth every Appointment of Chrift, though it be of perpetual Obligation, deferve the Name of a Sacrament: but thofe, and no other, which are,

4. Not only Signs of Grace, but *Means alfo, whereby we receive the fame*. None but our bleffed Lord could appoint fuch Means: and which of his Ordinances fhould be fuch, and which not, none but Himfelf could determine. From his Word therefore we are

LECTURE XXXIV.

to learn it: and then, as we hope to attain the End, we muſt uſe the Means. But when it is ſaid, that the Sacraments are Means of Grace; we are not to underſtand, either that the Performance of the mere outward Action doth, by its own Virtue, produce a ſpiritual Effect in us; or that God hath annexed any ſuch Effect to that alone: but that He will accompany the Action with his Bleſſing, provided it be done as it ought: with thoſe Qualifications which He requires. And therefore, unleſs we fulfil the Condition, we muſt not expect the Benefit.

Further; calling the Sacraments, Means of Grace, doth not ſignify them to be Means by which we merit Grace: for nothing but the Sufferings of our bleſſed Saviour can do that for us; but Means, by which what He hath merited is conveyed to us.

Nor yet are they the only Means of conveying Grace; for reading, and hearing, and meditating upon the Word of God, are Part of the Things which he hath appointed for this End; and Prayer is another Part, accompanied with an expreſs

Promise, that, *if we ask, we shall receive*[b]. But these, not being such Actions as figure out and represent the Benefits which they derive to us, though they are Means of Grace, are not Signs of it; and therefore do not come under the Notion of Sacraments. But,

5. A Sacrament is not only a Sign or Representation of some heavenly Favour, and a Means whereby we receive it, but also *a Pledge to assure us thereof.* Not that any Thing can give us a greater Assurance, in Point of Reason, of any Blessing from God, than his bare Promise can do: but that such Observances, appointed in Token of his Promises, affect our Imaginations with a stronger Sense of them: and make a deeper and more lasting, and therefore more useful Impression on our Minds. For this Cause, in all Nations of the World, Representations by Action have ever been used, as well as Words, upon solemn Occasions: especially upon entering into and renewing Treaties and Covenants with each other. And therefore, in Condescension to a Practice,

[b] John xvi. 24.

LECTURE XXXIV.

tice, which, being so universal among Men, appears to be founded in the Nature of Man; God hath graciously added to his Covenant also, the Solemnity of certain outward instructive Performances; by which he declares to us, that as surely as our Bodies are washed by Water, and nourished by Bread broken and Wine poured forth and received; so surely are our Souls purified from Sin by the Baptism of Repentance; and strengthened in all Goodness, by partaking of that Mercy, which the Wounding of the Body of Christ, and the Shedding of his Blood, hath obtained for us. And thus these religious Actions, so far as they are performed by God's Minister, in Pursuance of his Appointment, are an earnest or Pledge on his Part, which (as I observed to you) was one ancient Signification of the Word Sacrament: and so far as we join in them, they are an Obligation, binding like an Oath, on our Part, as shall be hereafter shewn you; which was the other primitive Meaning of the Word.

Having thus explained to you the Description of a Sacrament given in the Catechism;

chism; let us now consider, what Things we have in our Religion that answer to it. For the Papists reckon no less than seven Sacraments. And though this Number was not named for above 100 Years after Christ; nor fixed by the Authority of even their own Church, till 200 Years ago, that is, since the Reformation; yet now they accurse Us, for not agreeing with them in it, but acknowledging only two.

The first of their five is Confirmation. And if this be a Sacrament, we administer it as well as they, indeed much more agreeably to the original Practice; and are therefore intitled, at least, to the same Benefit from it. But though Christ did indeed *put his Hands on Children, and bless them*[c]; yet we do not read, that He appointed this particular Ceremony for a Means of conveying Grace. And though the Apostles did use it after Him, as others had done before Him; yet there is no Foundation to ascribe any separate Efficacy to the laying on of Hands, as distinct from the Prayers that accompany it: or to look upon the Whole

[c] Mark x. 16.

LECTURE XXXIV. 215

of Confirmation as any Thing elſe, than a ſolemn Manner of Perſons taking upon themſelves their baptiſmal Vow, followed by the ſolemn Addreſſes of the Biſhop and the Congregation, that they may ever keep it: in which Addreſſes, laying on of Hands is uſed, partly as a Mark of Good-Will to the Perſon for whom the Prayers are offered up; and partly alſo as a Sign, that the fatherly Hand of God is over all who undertake to ſerve Him; yet without any Claim of conveying his Grace particularly by it; but only with Intention of praying for his Grace along with it: which Prayers however we have ſo juſt Ground to hope he will hear, that they who neglect this Ordinance, though not a Sacrament, are greatly wanting both to their Intereſt and their Duty.

Another Sacrament of the Church of *Rome* is Penance; which they make to conſiſt of particular Confeſſion to the Prieſt of every deadly Sin, particularly Abſolution from him, and ſuch Acts of Devotion, Mortification, or Charity, as he ſhall think fit to enjoin. But no one Part of this being required

LECTURE XXXIV.

quired in Scripture, much less any outward Sign of it appointed, or any inward Grace annexed to it; there is nothing in the Whole that hath any Appearance of a Sacrament; but too much Suspicion of a Contrivance to gain undue Influence and Power.

A third Sacrament of theirs is, extreme Unction. But their Plea for it is no more than this. St. *James*, at a Time when miraculous Gifts were common, directed *the Elders of the Church*, who usually had those Gifts, to *anoint the Sick with Oil*[d]: as we read the Disciples did, whilst our Saviour was on Earth[e]; in order to obtain by the *Prayer of Faith*, (that *Faith* which could *remove Mountains*[f]) the Recovery, if God saw fit, of their bodily Health; and the Forgiveness of those Sins for which their Disease was inflicted, if they had committed any such. And upon this, the Church of *Rome*, now all such miraculous Gifts are ceased, continues notwithstanding to anoint the Sick, for a quite different Purpose: not at all for the Recovery of their Health;

---

[d] Jam. v. 14, 15.   [e] Mark vi. 13.   [f] Matth. xvii. 20. xxi 21. Mark x. 23.

LECTURE XXXIV.

for they do not ufe it till they think them very nearly, if not quite paft Recovery; nor indeed for the Pardon of their Sins, for thefe, they fay, are pardoned upon Confeffion, which commonly is made before it; but chiefly, as themfelves own, to procure Compofednefs and Courage in the Hour of Death: a Purpofe not only unmentioned by St. *James*, but inconfiftent with the Purpofe of Recovery, which he doth mention, and very often impoffible to be attained. For they frequently anoint Perfons after they are become intirely fenfelefs. And yet in Spite of all thefe Things, they will needs have this Practice owned for a Sacrament: which indeed is now, as they manage it, a mere Piece of Superftition.

Another Thing, which they efteem a Chriftian Sacrament, is Matrimony: though it was ordained, not by Chrift, but long before his Appearance on Earth, in the Time of Man's Innocency; and hath no outward Sign appointed in it, as a Means and Pledge of inward Grace. But the whole Matter is, that they have happened moft ridiculoufly to miftake their own Latin Tranflation of the New Teftament:

Testament: where St. *Paul*, having compared the Union between the first married Pair, *Adam* and *Eve*, to that between Christ, the second *Adam*, and his Spouse the Church; and having said that *this is a great Mystery*[g]; a Figure, or Comparison, not fully and commonly understood: the old Interpreter, whose Version they use, for *Mystery* hath put *Sacrament*: which in his Days, as I said before, signified any Thing in Religion that carried a hidden Meaning: and they have understood him of what we now call a Sacrament. Whereas if every Thing, that once had that Name in the largest Sense of the Word, were at present to have it in the stricter Sense; there would be a hundred Sacraments, instead of the seven, which they pretend there are.

The fifth and last Thing, which they wrongly insist on our honouring with this Title, is, holy Orders. But, as there are three Orders in the Church, Bishops, Priests, and Deacons; here would be three Sacraments, if there were any: but indeed there is none. For the laying on of Hands in Ordination is neither appointed nor used, to convey or signify any spiritual Grace

[g] Eph. v. 32.

LECTURE XXXIV.

Grace: but only to confer a Right of executing such an Office in the Church of Christ. And though Prayers, for God's Grace and Blessing on the Person ordained, are indeed very justly and usefully added; and will certainly be heard, unless the Person be unworthy: yet these Prayers, on this Occasion, no more make what is done a Sacrament, than any other Prayers for God's Grace, on any other Occasion.

However, as I have already said of Confirmation, so I say now of Orders and Marriage, if they were Sacraments, they would be as much so to us, as to the *Romanists*, whether we called them Sacraments, or not. And if we used the Name ever so erroneously, indeed if we never used it at all; as the Scripture hath never used it; that could do us no Harm, provided, under any Name, we believe but the Things, which Christ hath taught; and do but the Things which He hath commanded: for on this, and this alone, depends our Acceptance, and eternal Salvation.

LECTURE

LECTURE XXXV.

Of Baptism.

HAVING already explained to you the Nature of a Sacrament; and shewn you, that five of the seven Things, which the Church of *Rome* calls by that Name, are not ntitled to it; there remain only two, that are truly such: and these two are plainly sufficient: one, for our Entrance into the Christian Covenant; the other, during our whole Continuance in it: *Baptism, and the Supper of the Lord.* However, as the Word Sacrament is not a Scripture one, and hath at different Times been differently understood: our Catechism doth not require it to be said absolutely, that the Sacraments are *two only*; but *two only necessary to Salvation:* leaving Persons at Liberty to comprehend more Things under the Name if they please, provided they

insist

insist not on the Necessity of them, and of dignifying them with this Title. And even these two, our Church very charitably teaches us not to look upon as indispensably, but as *generally*, *necessary*. Out of which general Necessity, we are to except those particular Cases, where Believers in Christ, either have not the Means of performing their Duty in Respect to the Sacraments, or are innocently ignorant of it, or even excusably mistaken about it.

In explaining the Sacrament of *Baptism*, I shall speak, first of *the outward and visible Sign*, then of *the inward and spiritual Grace*.

As to the former: Baptism being intended for the Sign and Means of our Purification from Sin; Water, the proper Element for purifying and cleansing, is appointed to be used in it. There is indeed a Sect, sprung up amongst us within a little more than an hundred Years, that deny this Appointment: and make the Christian Baptism signify only the pouring out of the Gift of the Holy Ghost upon a Person. But our Saviour expressly requires that we be *born of Water*, as well as *of the Spirit*.

LECTURE XXXV.

Spirit, to *enter into the Kingdom of God*[a]. And not only *John*, his Forerunner, *baptized with Water*[b], but his *Disciples* also, by his Direction, *baptized* in the same Manner, even *more than John*[c]. When therefore He bad them afterwards *teach all Nations, baptizing them*[d]: what Baptism could they understand, but that, in which He had employed them before? And accordingly, we find, they did understand that. *Philip*, we read, baptized the Samaritans[e]: not with the Holy Ghost, for the Apostles went down some Time after to do that themselves[f]: but with Water undoubtedly, as we find in the same Chapter, he did the Enuch: where the Words are, *Here is Water: what doth hinder me to be baptized? And they went down to the Water: and he baptized him*[g]. Again, after *Cornelius*, and his Friends, had received the Holy Ghost, and so were already baptized in that Sense, *Peter* asks, *Can any Man forbid Water, that these should not be baptized, which have re-*

[a] John iii. 5. [b] Matth. iii. 11. [c] John iv. 1, 2.
[d] Matth. xxviii. 19. [e] Acts viii. 12. [f] Verse 14, &c.
[g] Verse 36, 38.

ceived the Holy Ghost, as well as we[h]? When therefore *John* says, that *He baptized with Water, but Christ shall baptize with the Holy Ghost*[i]; he means, not that Christians should not be baptized with Water, but that they should have the Holy Ghost poured out upon them also, in a Degree that *John's* Disciples had not. When St. *Peter* says, *The Baptism, which saveth us, is not the washing away the Filth of the Flesh*[k]; he means, it is not the mere outward Act, unaccompanied by a suitable inward Disposition. When St. *Paul* says, that *Christ sent him not to baptize, but to preach the Gospel*[l]; he means, that preaching was the principal Thing he was to do in Person: to baptize, he might appoint others under him; and it seems, commonly did: as St. *Peter* did dot baptize *Cornelius* and his Friends himself, but *commanded them to be babtized*[m]; and we read in St. *John*, that *Jesus baptized not, but his Disciples*[n].

Water-Baptism therefore is appointed, And why the Church of *Rome* should not

[h] Acts x. 47.   [i] Matth. iii. 11.   [k] 1 Pet. iii. 21.
[l] 1 Cor. i. 17.   [m] Acts x. 48.   [n] John iv. 2.

think

LECTURE XXXV.

think Water sufficient in Baptism, but aim at mending what our Saviour hath directed, by mixing Oil and Balsam with it, and dipping a lighted Torch into it, I leave them to explain.

The precise Manner, in which Water shall be applied in Baptism, Scripture hath not determined. For the Word, *baptize*, means only to wash: whether that be done by plunging a Thing under Water, or pouring the Water upon it. The former of these; burying, as it were, the Person baptized, in the Water, and raising him out of it again, without Question was anciently the more usual Method: on Account of which, St. *Paul* speaks of Baptism, as representing both the Death, and Burial, and Resurrection of Christ, and what is grounded on them, our being *dead and buried to Sin*; renouncing it, and being acquitted of it; and our rising again, to *walk in Newness of Life*[o]; being both obliged and enabled to practise, for the future, every Duty of Piety and Virtue. But still the other Manner of washing, by pouring or sprinkling of Wa-

[o] Rom. vi. 4, 11. Col. ii. 12.

ter,

ter, sufficiently expresses the same two Things: our being by this Ordinance purified from the Guilt of Sin, and bound and qualified to keep ourselves pure from the Defilement of it. Besides, it very naturally represents that *Sprinkling of the Blood of Jesus Christ* [p], to which our Salvation is owing. And the Use of it seems not only to be foretold by the Prophet *Isaiah*, speaking of our Saviour, *He shall sprinkle many Nations* [q], that is, many shall receive his Baptism; and by the Prophet *Ezekiel*, *Then will I sprinkle clean Water upon you, and ye shall be clean* [r]: but to be had in View also by the Apostle, where he speaks of *having our Hearts sprinkled from an evil Conscience, and our Bodies washed with pure Water* [s]. And though it was less frequently used in the first Ages, it must almost of Necessity have been sometimes used: for Instance, when Baptism was administered, as we read in the Acts it was, to several Thousands at once [t]; when it was administered on a sudden in private Houses, as we find it, in the same Book,

[p] 1 Pet. i. 2.   [q] Isaiah lii. 15.   [r] Ezek. xxxvi. 25.
[s] Heb. x. 22.   [t] Acts ii. 41.

LECTURE XXXV.

to the Goaler and all his Family, the very Night in which they were converted[u]: or when sick Persons received it; in which last Case, the present Method was always taken, because the other of dipping them, might have been dangerous. And from the same Apprehension of Danger in these colder Countries, pouring the Water is allowed, even when the Person baptized is in Health. And the particular Manner being left at Liberty, that is now universally chosen, which is looked on as safer: because were there more to be said for the other, than there is; God *will have Mercy, and not Sacrifice*[w].

But washing with Water is not the whole outward Part of this Sacrament. For our Saviour commanded his Apostles, not only to *baptize all Nations,* but to *baptize them in the Name of the Father, and of the Son, and of the Holy Ghost*[x]. Sometimes indeed the Scripture speaks of Baptism, as if it were administered only *in the Name of the Lord Jesus*[y]. But it fully ap-

[u] Acts xvi. 33.   [w] Hos. vi. 6. Matth. ix. 13. xii. 7.
[x] Matth. xxviii. 19.   [y] Acts ii. 38. x. 48. xix. 5.

pears,

pears [z], that the Name of the Holy Ghost; was used at the same Time: and therefore that of the Father, we may be sure. Now being baptized *in the Name* of these Three may signify, being baptized by Virtue of their Authority. But the exacter Translation is, *into the Name:* and the fuller Import of the Expression is, by this solemn Action taking upon us their Name; (for Servants are known by the Name of their Master) and professing ourselves devoted to the Faith, and Worship, and Obedience of these Three; our Creator, our Redeemer, our Sanctifier. In this Profession, the whole of Christianity is briefly comprehended, and on this Foundation therefore the ancient Creeds are all built.

The second and principal Thing in Baptism, *the inward and spiritual Grace*, is said in the Catechism to be, *a Death unto Sin, and a new Birth unto Righteousness: for that being by Nature born in Sin, and the Children of Wrath, we are hereby made the Children of Grace.* The former Part of these Words refers to the old Custom of baptizing by

[z] Acts xix. 2, 3.

dipping,

dipping, just now mentioned: and the Meaning of the whole is this. Our first Parents, having, by Disobedience in eating the forbidden Fruit, corrupted their own Nature; ours, being derived from them, received of Necessity an original Taint of the same Disorder: and therefore coming into the World under the ill Effects of their Sin; and being, from the Time of our entering into it, prone to sin ourselves: we are said to be *born in Sin*. And they having also, by the same Disobedience, forfeited their Immortality; we, as descending from them, became mortal of Course: and inheriting by way of natural Consequence, what they suffered as a Mark of God's Wrath; we, their Children, are said to be *Children of Wrath*. Not that God, with whatever Disapprobation He must view our native Depravity, is, or, properly speaking, can be angry with us personally, for what was not our personal Fault. But He might undoubtedly both refuse us that Immortality, which our first Parents had forfeited, and to which we have no Right; and leave us without Help, to the poor Degree of

Strength,

Strength, that remained to us in our fallen Condition; the Effect of which must have been; that had we done our best, as we were intitled to no Reward from his Justice, so it had been such a Nothing, that we could have hoped for little, if any, from his Bounty: and had we not done our best, as no Man hath, we had no Assurance, that even Repentance would secure us from Punishment. But what in strict Justice He might have done, in his infinite Goodness He hath not done. For the first Covenant being broken by *Adam*, He hath entered into a new one with Mankind, through Jesus Christ: in which He hath promised to free us, both from the Mortality, which our first Parents had brought upon us, by restoring us to Life again; and from the Inability, by the powerful Assistance of his Holy Spirit. Nay further yet, He hath promised, (and without it the rest would have been of small Use) that should we, notwithstanding his Assistance, fail in our Duty, when we might have performed it; as we have all failed, and made ourselves, by that Means, *Children of Wrath*, in the

strictest

LECTURE XXXV.

stricteſt and worſe Senſe: yet, on moſt equitable Terms, He would ſtill receive us to Mercy anew. And thus the Chriſtian Covenant, delivering us, if we are faithful to it, from every Thing we had to fear, and beſtowing on us every Thing we could hope, brings us into a State ſo unſpeakably different from our former; that it is juſtly expreſſed by being dead to that, and born into another. And this new Birth being effected by the Grace or Goodneſs of God, external and internal, we, the Children of it, are properly called *the Children of Grace.* Now Baptiſm is not only a Sign of this Grace; (as indeed it ſignifies very naturally the waſhing off both of our original Corruption, and our actual Guilt) but the appointed Way of entering into the Covenant that intitles us to ſuch Grace; the *Means whereby we receive the ſame, and a Pledge to aſſure us thereof.*

Indeed the mere outward Act of being baptized is, as St. *Peter,* in the Words already mentioned, very truly expreſſes it, the mere *putting away of the Filth of the Fleſh;* unleſs it be made effectual to ſave us, as he

teaches

teaches in the same Place it must, by *the Answer of a good Conscience towards God*[a]: that is, by the sincere Stipulation and Engagement of *Repentance, whereby we forsake Sin; and Faith, whereby we believe the Promises of God, made to us in that Sacrament.* For it is impossible that He should forgive us our past Sins, unless we are sorry for them, and resolved to quit them: and it is as impossible that we should quit them effectually, unless a firm Persuasion of his helping and rewarding us excite and support our Endeavours. These two Things therefore we see our Catechism justly mentions as necessary, in Answer to the Question, *What is required of Persons to be baptized?* Both have been explained in their proper Place, and therefore I enlarge on neither here.

But hence arises immediately another Question: If these Conditions are necessary, *why are Infants baptized, when by Reason of their tender Age they cannot perform them?* And as this Difficulty appears to some a great one, I shall give a fuller Solution of it than the Shortness of a Catechism would easily

[a] 1 Pet. iii. 21.

permit,

LECTURE XXXV.

permit. Repentance and Faith are requisite, not before they are possible, but when they are possible. Repentance is what Infants need not as yet, being clear of personal Guilt: and happy would it be, were they never to need it. Faith, it may be reasonably presumed, by the Security given for their Christian Education, they will have, as soon as they have Occasion to exert it. And in the mean Time, Baptism may very fitly be administered: because God, on his Part, can certainly express by it, both his removing, at present, the Disadvantages which they lie under by the Sin of *Adam:* and his removing hereafter, on proper Conditions, the Disadvantages which they may come to lie under by their own Sins. And though they cannot, on their Parts, expressly promise to perform these Conditions; yet they are not only bound to perform them, whether they promise it or not; but (which is the Point that our Catechism insists on) their Sureties promise for them, that they shall be made sensible, as soon as may be, that they are so bound; and ratify the Engagement in their own Persons,

which

which when they do, it then becomes complete. For it is by no Means necessary, that a Covenant should be executed, by both the Parties to it, at just the same Time: and as the Christian Covenant is one of the greatest Equity and Favour, we cannot *doubt*, to speak in the Language of our Liturgy, *but that God favourably alloweth the charitable Work of bringing Infants to his holy Baptism.* For *the Promise* of the Covenant being expresly said to belong *to us and to our Children* [b], without any Limitation of Age; why should they not all, since they are to partake of the Promise, partake also of the Sign of it? especially, since the Infants of the Jews were, by a solemn Sign, entered into their Covenant; and the Infants of Proselytes to the Jews, by this very Sign, amongst others, of Baptism. So that, supposing the Apostles to imitate either of these Examples, as they naturally would, unless they were forbidden, which they were not: when they baptized (as the Scripture, without making any Exception, tells us they did) whole Families at once [c];

[b] Acts ii. 39. [c] Acts xvi. 15. 33.

we

LECTURE XXXV.

we cannot question but they baptized (as we know the primitive Christians, their Successors, did) *little Children* amongst the rest; concerning whom our Saviour says, that *of such is the Kingdom of God*[d]: and St. Paul says, *they are holy*[e]; which they cannot be reputed, without entering into the Gospel Covenant: and the only appointed Way of entering into it is by Baptism; which therefore is constantly represented in the New Testament as necessary to Salvation.

Not that such Converts, in ancient Times, as were put to Death for their Faith, before they could be baptized, lost their Reward for Want of it. Not that such Children of Believers now, as die unbaptized by sudden Illness, or unexpected Accidents, or even by Neglect, (since it is none of their own Neglect) shall forfeit the Advantages of Baptism. This would be very contrary to that Mercy and Grace, which abounds through the whole of the Gospel Dispensation. Nay, where the Persons themselves do designedly, through mistaken Notions,

[d] Mark x. 14.   [e] 1 Cor. vii. 14.

either

either delay their Baptism, as the Anabaptists; or omit it intirely, as the Quakers; even of these it belongs to Christian Charity not to judge hardly, as excluded from the Gospel Covenant, if they die unbaptized; but to leave them to the equitable Judgment of God. Both of them indeed err: and the latter especially have, one should think, as little Excuse for their Error as well can be: for surely there is no Duty of Christianity which stands on a plainer Foundation, than that of baptizing with Water in the Name of the Holy Trinity. But still, since they solemnly declare, that they believe in Christ, and desire to obey his Commands; and omit Water-Baptism only because they cannot see it is commanded; we ought (if we have Cause to think they speak Truth) by no Means to consider them in the same Light with total Unbelievers.

But the wilful and the careless Despisers of this Ordinance: who, admitting it to be of God's Appointment, neglect it notwithstanding; these are not to be looked on as within his Covenant. And such as, though they do observe it for Form's Sake, treat it

as

LECTURE XXXV.

as an empty infignificant Ceremony, are very unworthy of the Benefits which it was intended to convey. And, bad as thefe Things are, little better, if not worfe, will be the Cafe of thofe, who, acknowledging the folemn Engagements into which they have entered by this Sacrament, live without Care to make them good. For to the only valuable Purpofe, of God's Favour and eternal Happinefs, *He is not a* Chriftian, *which is one outwardly; neither is that* Baptifm *which is outward in the Flefh: but He is a* Chriftian, *which is one inwardly; and* Baptifm *is that of the Heart, in the Spirit, and not in the Letter; whofe Praife is not of Men, but of God*[f].

[f] Rom. ii. 28, 29.

LECTURE XXXVI.

Of the LORD's SUPPER.

PART I.

AS by the Sacrament of Baptism we enter into the Christian Covenant; so by that of the Lord's Supper we profess our thankful Continuance in it: and therefore the first Answer of our Catechism, concerning this Ordinance, tells us, it was appointed *For the continual Remembrance of the Sacrifice of the Death of Christ, and of the Benefits which we receive thereby.* Now the Nature and Benefits of this Sacrifice have been already explained, in their proper Places. I shall therefore proceed to shew, that the Lord's Supper is rightly said here to be *ordained for a Remembrance* of it; not a Repetition, as the Church of *Rome* teaches.

Indeed

Indeed every Act, both of Worship and Obedience, is in some Sense a Sacrifice to God, humbly offered up to Him for his Acceptance. And this Sacrament in particular, being a Memorial and Representation of the Sacrifice of Christ, solemnly and religiously made, may well enough be called, in a figurative Way of speaking, by the same Name with what it commemorates and represents. But that he should be really and literally offered up in it, is the directest Contradiction that can be, not only to Common Sense, but also to Scripture, which expressly says, that He was not to be *offered often, for then must He often have suffered; but hath appeared once to put away Sin by the Sacrifice of Himself*[a], and after that *for ever sat down on the right Hand of God: for by one Offering He hath perfected for ever them that are sanctified*[b].

This Ordinance then was appointed, not to repeat, but to commemorate the Sacrifice of Christ; which though we are required to do, and do accordingly, more or less explicitly, in all our Acts of Devotion, yet we are not

[a] Heb. ix. 25, 26.   [b] Heb. x. 12, 14.

required

LECTURE XXXVI.

required to do it by any visible Representation, but that of the Lord's Supper: of which therefore our Catechism teaches, in the second Answer, that *the outward Part, or Sign, is Bread and Wine, which the Lord hath commanded to be received.* And indeed he hath so clearly commanded both to be received, that no reasonable Defence in the least can be made, either for the Sect usually called Quakers, who omit this Sacrament entirely; or for the Church of *Rome,* who deprive the Laity of one half of it, the Cup; and forbid all but the Priest to do, what Christ hath appointed all without Exception to do. They plead indeed, that all, whom Christ appointed to receive the Cup; that is, the Apostles; were Priests. But their Church forbids the Priests themselves to receive it, excepting those who perform the Service: which the Apostles did not perform, but their Master. And besides, if the Appointment of receiving the Cup belongs only to Priests, that of receiving the Bread too must relate only to Priests: for our Saviour hath more expresly directed *all* to drink of the one, than to eat of the other.

other. But they own, that his Appointment obliges the Laity to receive the Bread: and therefore it obliges them to receive the Cup alfo: which that they did accordingly, 1 *Cor.* xi. makes as plain as Words can make any Thing: nor was it refufed them for 1200 Years after. They plead farther, that adminiftering the holy Sacrament is called in Scripture *breaking of Bread,* without mentioning the Cup at all. And we allow it. But when common Feafts are expreffed in Scripture by the fingle Phrafe of *eating Bread,* furely this doth not prove that the Guefts drank nothing: and if, in this religious Feaft, the like Phrafe could prove, that the Laity did not partake of the Cup, it will prove equally, that the Priefts did not partake of it either. They plead in the laft Place, that by receiving the Bread, which is the Body of Chrift, we receive in Effect the Cup, which is the Blood, at the fame Time: for the Blood is contained in the Body. But here, befides that our Saviour, who was furely the beft Judge, appointed both; they quite forget, that this Sacrament is a Memorial of his Blood

LECTURE XXXVI.

Blood being shed out of his Body: of which, without the Cup, there can be no Commemoration: or, if there could, the Cup would be as needless for the Clergy as for the Laity.

The outward Signs therefore, which Christ hath commanded to be received, equally received by all Christians, are Bread and Wine. Of these the *Jews* had been accustomed to partake, in a serious and devout Manner, at all their Feasts, after a solemn Blessing, or Thanksgiving to God, made over them, for his Goodness to Men. But especially at the Feast of the Passover, which our Saviour was celebrating with his Disciples, when he instituted this holy Sacrament; at that Feast, in the abovementioned Thanksgiving, they commemorated more at large the Mercies of their God, dwelling chiefly however on their Deliverance from the Bondage of *Egypt*. Now this having many Particulars resembling that infinitely more important Redemption of all Mankind from Sin and Ruin, which our Saviour was then about to accomplish; He very naturally directed his Disciples, that their ancient Custom should for the future be applied to this greatest of divine Blessings, and become the Memorial of *Christ, their Passover, sacrificed for them*[c]: as indeed the Bread broken aptly enough represented his Body; and the Wine poured forth most expressively figured out his Blood, shed for our Salvation. These therefore, as the third Answer of our Catechism very justly teaches, are *the inward Part* of this Sacrament, *or the Thing signified*.

But the Church of *Rome*, instead of being content with saying, that the Bread and Wine are Signs of the Body and Blood of Christ, insist on it, that they are turned into the very Substance of his Body and Blood: which imagined Change they therefore call Transubstantiation. Now were this true, there would be no outward Sign left: for they say, it is converted into the Thing signified: and by Consequence there would be no Sacrament left: for a Sacrament is *an outward Sign of an inward Grace*.

Besides, if our Senses can in any Case inform us what any Thing is, they inform us,

[c] 1 Cor. v. 7.

that

LECTURE XXXVI.

that the Bread and Wine continue Bread and Wine. And if we cannot truſt our Senſes, when we have full Opportunity of uſing them all; how did the Apoſtles know that our Saviour taught them, and performed Miracles; or how do we know any one Thing around us? But this Doctrine is equally contrary to all Reaſon too. To believe that our Saviour took his own Body, literally ſpeaking, in his own Hands, and gave the whole of that one Body to every one of his Apoſtles, and that each of them ſwallowed Him down their Throats, though all the while He continued ſitting at the Table before their Eyes: to believe, that the very ſame one individual Body, which is now in Heaven, is alſo in many thouſands of different Places on Earth; in ſome, ſtanding ſtill upon the Altar; in others, carrying along the Streets; and ſo in Motion, and not in Motion, at the ſame Time: to believe, that the ſame Body can come from a great Diſtance, and meet itſelf, as the ſacramental Bread often doth in their Proceſſions, and then paſs by itſelf, and go away from itſelf to the ſame Diſtance again;

again; is to believe the moſt abſolute Impoſſibilities and Contradictions. If ſuch Things can be true, nothing can be falſe; and if ſuch Things cannot be true, the Church that teaches them cannot be infallible, whatever Arts of puzzling Sophiſtry they may uſe to prove either that or any of their Doctrines. For no Reaſonings are ever to be minded againſt plain Common Senſe.

They muſt not ſay, this Doctrine is a Myſtery. For there is no Myſtery, no Obſcurity in it: but it is as plainly ſeen to be an Error, as any Thing elſe is ſeen to be a Truth. And the more ſo, becauſe it relates, not to an infinite Nature, as God; but entirely to what is finite, a Bit of Bread and a human Body. They muſt not plead, that God can do all Things. For that means only that He can do all Things that can be done: not that He can do what cannot be done; make a Thing be this and not be this, be here and elſewhere, at the ſame Time: which is doing and undoing at once, and ſo in Reality doing nothing. They muſt not alledge Scripture for Abſurdities, that would

LECTURE XXXVI.

would sooner prove Scripture false, than Scripture can prove them true. But it no where teaches them.

We own that our Saviour says, *This is my Body, which is broken* [d], and, *This is my Blood, which is shed* [e]. But he could not mean literally. For as yet his Body was not broken, nor his Blood shed: nor is either of them in that Condition now. And therefore the Bread and Wine neither could then, nor can now, be turned into them, as such. Besides, our Saviour said at the same Time, *This Cup is the New Testament in my Blood* [f]. Was the Substance of the Cup then changed into the New Testament? And if not, why are we to think the Substance of the Bread and Wine changed into his Body and Blood? The Apostle says, *the Rock*, that supplied the *Israelites* with Water in the Wilderness, *was Christ* [g]: that is, represented Him. Every Body says such a Picture is such a Person, meaning the Representation of him. Why then may not our Saviour's Words mean so too?

[d] 1 Cor. xi. 24.   [e] Matth. xxvi. 28.   [f] Luke xxii. 20.
1 Cor. xi. 25.   [g] 1 Cor. x. 4.

LECTURE XXXVI.

The *Romanists* object, that though what represents a Thing naturally, or by Virtue of a preceding Institution, may be called by its Name, yet such a Figure as this, in the Words of a new Institution, would not be intelligible [h]. But the Representation here is natural enough: and though the Institution was new, figurative Speech was old. And the Apostles would certainly rather interpret their Master's Words by a very usual Figure, than put the absurdest Sense upon them that could be. They object further, that if He had not meant literally, He would have said, not, *This*, but *This Bread*, is my Body [i]. But we may better argue, that if He had meant literally, He would have said, in the strongest Terms, that He did. For there was great Need, surely, of such a Declaration. But we acknowledge, that the Bread and Wine are more than a Representation of his Body and Blood: they are the Means, by which the Benefits, arising from them, are conveyed to us; and have thence a further Title

[h] Preuves de la Religion, Vol. IV. p. 166.   [i] Ib. p. 168.

LECTURE XXXVI.

to be called by their Name. For so the Instrument, by which a Prince forgives an Offender, is called his Pardon, because it conveys his Pardon; the Delivery of a Writing is called giving Possession of an Estate[k]; and a Security for a Sum of Money, is called the Sum itself; and is so in Virtue and Effect, though it is not in Strictness of Speech, and Reality of Substance. Again: our Saviour, we own, says in St. *John*, that *He is the Bread of Life;* that *his Flesh is Meat indeed, and his Blood is Drink indeed: that whoso eateth the one and drinketh the other, hath eternal Life;* and that, without doing it, *we have no Life in us*[l]. But this, if understood literally, would prove, not that the Bread in the Sacrament was turned into his Flesh, but that his Flesh was turned into Bread. And therefore it is not to be understood literally, as indeed He himself gives Notice: *The Flesh profiteth nothing: the Words which I speak unto you, they are Spirit and they are Life*[m]: It is not the gross and literal, but the figurative and spiritual, eating and drinking; the partaking by a lively

[k] See Cod. 8. 54. 1. [l] John vi. 48, 53, 54, 55. [m] Ver. 63.

Faith

Faith of an Union with me, and being inwardly nourished by the Fruits of my offering up my Flesh and Blood for you, that alone can be of Benefit to the Soul.

And as this is plainly the Sense, in which He says, that *his Flesh is Meat indeed, and his Blood is Drink indeed:* so it is the Sense, in which the latter Part of the third Answer of our Catechism is to be understood; that *the Body and Blood of Christ are verily and indeed taken and received by the Faithful in the Lord's Supper:* Words intended to shew, that our Church as truly believes the strongest Assurances of Scripture concerning this Sacrament, as the Church of *Rome* doth; only takes more Care to understand them in the right Meaning: which is, that though, in one Sense, all Communicants equally partake of what Christ calls his Body and Blood, that is, the outward Signs of them; yet in a much more important Sense, *the Faithful* only, the pious and virtuous Receiver, eats his Flesh and drinks his Blood; shares in the Life and Strength derived to Men from his Incarnation and Death; and through Faith in

LECTURE XXXVI.

in Him, becomes, by a vital Union, one with Him; *a Member*, as St. *Paul* expresses it, *of his Flesh and his Bones*[n]: certainly not in a literal Sense; which yet the *Romanists* might as well assert, as that we eat his Flesh in a literal Sense; but in a figurative and spiritual one. In Appearance, the Sacrament of Christ's Death is given to all alike: but *verily and indeed*, in its beneficial Effects, to none besides the Faithful. Even to the unworthy Communicant He is present, as He is wherever we meet together in his Name: but in a better and most gracious Sense, to the worthy Soul; becoming, by the inward Virtue of his Spirit, its Food and Sustenance.

This real Presence of Christ in the Sacrament, his Church hath always believed. But the monstrous Notion of his bodily Presence was started 700 Years after his Death: and arose chiefly from the Indiscretion of Preachers and Writers of warm Imaginations, who, instead of explaining judiciously the lofty Figures of Scripture-Language, heightened them, and went be-

[n] Eph. v. 30.

yond

yond them: till both it and they had their Meaning mistaken most astonishingly. And when once an Opinion had taken Root, that seemed to exalt the holy Sacrament so much, it easily grew and spread; and the more for its wonderful Absurdity, in those ignorant and superstitious Ages: till at length, 500 Years ago, and 1200 Years after our Saviour's Birth, it was established for a Gospel-Truth by the pretended Authority of the *Romish* Church. And even this had been tolerable in Comparison, if they had not added idolatrous Practice to erroneous Belief: worshipping, on their Knees, a Bit of Bread for the Son of God. Nor are they content to do this themselves, but with most unchristian Cruelty, curse and murder those, who refuse it.

It is true, we also kneel at the Sacrament, as they do: but for a very different Purpose: not to acknowledge *any corporal Presence of Christ's natural Flesh and Blood*; as our Church, to prevent all Possibility of Misconstruction, expressly declares; adding, that *his Body is in Heaven, and not here:* but to worship Him, who is every where present,

LECTURE XXXVI.

present, the invisible God. And this Posture of kneeling we by no Means look upon, as in itself necessary; but as a very becoming Appointment; and very fit to accompany the Prayers and Praises, which we offer up at the Instant of receiving; and to express that inward Spirit of Piety and Humility, on which our partaking worthily of this Ordinance, and receiving Benefit from it, depend. But the Benefits of the holy Sacrament, and the Qualifications for it, shall, God willing, be the Subject of two other Discourses. In the mean Time, *consider what hath been said; and the Lord give you Understanding in all Things*[o].

[o] 2 Tim. ii. 7.

LECTURE XXXVII.

Of the LORD's SUPPER.

PART II.

THE Doctrine of our Catechism, concerning the Lord's Supper, hath been already so far explained, as to shew you, that it *was ordained, not for* the Repetition, but *the continual Remembrance of the Sacrifice of Christ*; that *the outward Signs* in it are *Bread and Wine*; both *which the Lord hath commanded to be received* by all Christians: and both which are accordingly received, and not changed and transubstantiated into the real and natural *Body and Blood of Christ:* which however *the Faithful*, and they only, do, under this Representation of it, *verily and indeed* receive into a most beneficial Union with themselves;

that

that is, do *verily and indeed*, by a spiritual Connection with their incarnate Redeemer and Head through Faith, partake, in this Ordinance, of that heavenly Favour and Grace, which by offering up his Body and Blood he hath procured for his true Disciples and Members.

But of *what Benefit* in particular *the Faithful* partake in this Sacrament through the Grace and Favour of God, our Catechism teaches in the fourth Answer, to which I now proceed: and which tells us it is, *The strengthening and refreshing of our Souls by the Body and Blood of Christ, as our Bodies are by the Bread and Wine*[a]: Now both the Truth and the Manner of this Refreshment of our Souls will appear by considering the Nature of the Sacrament, and the Declarations of Scripture concerning it.

Indeed the due Preparation for it, the Self-examination required in order to it, and the religious Exercises which that Ex-

---

[a] Αλλα πασασθαι ανωχθι θοης επι νηυσιν ΑχαιȢς Σιτȣ και οινοιο· το γαρ μενος εςι και αλκη.
HOM. IL. T. v. 160, 161.

amination

amination will of Courſe point out to us, muſt previouſly be of great Service; as you will ſee, when I come to that Head. And the actual Participation will add further Advantages of unſpeakable Value.

Conſidered as an act of Obedience to our Saviour's Command, *Do this in Remembrance of me*, it muſt be beneficial to us: for all Obedience will. Conſidered as Obedience to a Command, proceeding principally, if not ſolely, from his mere Will and Pleaſure; it contributes to form us into a very needful, a ſubmiſſive and implicitly dutiful, Temper of Mind. But further: it is the moſt eminent and diſtinguiſhed Act of Chriſtian Worſhip: conſiſting of the devouteſt Thankfulneſs to God for the greateſt Bleſſing, which He ever beſtowed on Man; attended, as it naturally muſt, with earneſt Prayers, that the Gift may avail us, to our ſpiritual and eternal Good. And it is much more likely to affect us very ſtrongly and uſefully, becauſe it expreſſes his Bounty and our Senſe of it, not as our daily Devotions do, in Words alone, but in the leſs common, and therefore more ſolemn Way, of viſible

Signs and Representations: *setting forth evidently before our Eyes*, to use St. *Paul's* Language, *Christ crucified among st us* [b]. This, of Necessity, unless we are strangely wanting to ourselves, must raise the warmest Affections of Love, that our Hearts are capable of, to Him who hath given his Son, to Him who hath given Himself for us. And as Love is the noblest Principle of religious Behaviour, what tends so powerfully to animate our Love, must in Proportion tend to perfect us in every Branch of Duty, according to the just Reasoning of the same Apostle: *For the Love of Christ constraineth us; because we thus judge, that if one died for all, then were all dead; and He died for all, that they who live, should not henceforth live unto themselves, but unto Him, which died for them, and rose again* [c]. When our Saviour said to his Disciples, *If ye love me, keep my Commandments* [d]; He knew the Motive was no less engaging, than it is reasonable. And therefore He adds very soon after, *If a Man love me, he will keep my Words* [e].

[b] Gal. iii. 1.   [c] 2 Cor. v. 15, 16.   [d] John xiv. 15.
[e] Ver. 23.

LECTURE XXXVII.

But this Institution carries in it a yet further Tye upon us; being, as our blessed Lord himself declared, *the New Testament in his Blood*[f]: the Memorial and Acknowledgment of the second Covenant between God and Man, which was founded on his Death; and requires a sincere Faith and Obedience on our Part, as the Condition of Grace and Mercy on his, *Every one, that nameth the Name of Christ, is bound to depart from Iniquity*[g]. But the Obligation is redoubled on them who come to his Table as Friends, and *make a Covenant with Him by* partaking of his *Sacrifice*[h]. If these live wickedly, it is declaring with the boldest Contempt, that they consider *Christ* as *the Minister of Sin*[i]; and *count the Blood of the Covenant*, wherewith they profess to be *sanctified, an unholy Thing*[k]. Partaking therefore of his holy Ordinance is renewing, in the most awful Manner, our Engagements to the Service which we owe, as well as our Claims to the Favours, that God hath promised. It is our Sacrament,

[f] Luke xxii. 20.   [g] 2 Tim. ii. 19.   [h] Psalm l. 5.
[i] Gal. ii. 17.   [k] Heb. x. 29.

our Oath to be faithful *Soldiers*[1] under *the great Captain of our Salvation*[m]: which surely we cannot take thus, without being efficaciously influenced to the religious Observances of it, in every Part of a Christian Life.

But there is one Part especially, and one of the utmost Importance, to which this Institution peculiarly binds us, that of universal Good-will and Charity. For commemorating, in so solemn an Action, the Love of Christ to us all, cannot but move us to that mutual Imitation of his Love, which, just before his appointing this holy Sacrament, He so earnestly and effectionately enjoined his Followers, as the distinguishing Badge of their Profession. *This is my Commandment, that ye love one another, as I have loved you. Greater Love hath no Man than this, that a Man lay down his Life for his Friends. Ye are my Friends, if ye do whatsoever I command you*[n]. *Hereby shall all Men know, that ye are my Disciples, if ye have Love one to another*[o]. Then besides;

[1] 2 Tim. ii. 3, 4. [m] Heb. ii. 10. [n] John xv. 12, 13, 14. [o] John xiii. 35.

commemorating

commemorating his Love jointly, as the Servants of one Mafter, and Members of one Body, partaking of the fame Covenant of Grace, and the fame Hope of everlafting Happinefs, muft, if we have any Feeling of what we do, incline us powerfully to that reciprocal Union of Hearts, which indeed the very act of communicating fuggefts and recommends to us. *For we, being many, are one Bread and one Body: for we are all Partakers of that one Bread* [p].

Another Grace, which this Commemoration of our Saviour's Death peculiarly excites, is Humility of Soul. We acknowledge by it, that we are Sinners; and have no Claim to Pardon or Acceptance, but through his Sacrifice, and his Mediation, whofe Merits we thus plead, and fet forth before God. And this Confideration muft furely difpofe us very ftrongly to a thankful Obfervance of his Commands, to Watchfulnefs over our own Hearts, to Mildnefs towards others. *For we ourfelves alfo have been foolifh, difobedient, deceived: and not by Works of Righteoufnefs, which we have*

[p] 1 Cor. x, 17.

done,

done, but according to his Mercy, God hath saved us, which He shed on us abundantly through Christ Jesus our Saviour [q].

And as this Sacrament will naturally strengthen us in all these good Dispositions, we cannot doubt, but God will add his Blessing to the Use of such proper Means, especially being appointed Means. For since he hath threatened Punishments to unworthy Receivers, He will certainly bestow Rewards on worthy ones. Our Saviour hath told us, that *his Flesh is Meat indeed, and his Blood is Drink indeed*[r]: Sustenance and Refreshment to the Souls of Men. When He blessed the Bread and Wine, He undoubtedly prayed, and not in vain, that they might be effectual for the good Purposes, which He designed should be attained by this holy Rite. And St. *Paul* hath told us, if it needs, more expresly, that *the Cup, which we bless, is the Communion*, that is, the Communication to us, *of the Blood of Christ; and the Bread, which we break, of the Body of Christ*[s]: that is, of a saving Union with Him, and therefore of

[q] Tit. iii. 3, 5, 6. [r] John vi. 55. [s] 1 Cor. x. 16.

the

LECTURE XXXVII.

the Benefits procured to us by his Death: which are, Forgiveneſs of our Offences; for He hath ſaid, *This is my Blood of the New Teſtament, which is ſhed for the Remiſſion of Sins*[t]*:* Increaſe of the gracious Influences of the Holy Ghoſt; for the Apoſtle hath ſaid, plainly ſpeaking of this Ordinance, that *we are all made to drink into one Spirit*[u]*:* and everlaſting Life; for *whoſo eateth his Fleſh, and drinketh his Blood, dwelleth in Chriſt, and Chriſt in him, and He will raiſe him up at the laſt Day*[w]. Whence a Father of the apoſtolic Age, *Ignatius,* calls the Euchariſt, *the Medicine of Immortality; a Preſervative, that we ſhould not die, but live for ever in Jeſus Chriſt*[x].

But then what hath been already hinted to you muſt be always carefully obſerved; that theſe Benefits are to be expected only from partaking worthily of it: *for he that eateth and drinketh unworthily,* St. *Paul* hath told us, *is guilty of the Body and Blood of the Lord*[y], that is, guilty of Irreverence to-

[t] Matth. xxvi. 28.   [u] 1 Cor. xii. 13.   [w] John vi. 54, 56.
[x] Ign. ad Eph. c. 20.   See Waterland on the Euchariſt, p. 217.   [y] 1 Cor. xi. 27.

wards it, and *eateth and drinketh Judgment to himself*[z]. Our Translation indeed hath it, *Damnation to himself*. But there is so great Danger of this last Word being understood here in too strong a Sense, that it would be much safer, and exacter, to translate it, (as it is often translated elsewhere, and once in a few Verses after this Passage, and from what follows ought undeniably to be translated here) *Judgment* or *Condemnation:* not to certain Punishment in another Life, but to such Marks of God's Displeasure as He sees fit; which will be confined to this World, or extended to the next, as the Case requires. For *receiving unworthily* may, according to the Kind and Degree of it, be either a very great Sin, or comparatively a small one. But all dangerous Kinds and Degrees may with Ease be avoided, if we only take Care to come to the Sacrament with proper Dispositions, and, which will follow of Course, to behave at it in a proper Manner.

[z] 1 Cor. xi. 29.

LECTURE XXXVII.

To these Dispositions our Catechism proceeds. But more is needful to be known concerning them than can well be laid before you now. Therefore I shall conclude at present with desiring you to observe, that no Unworthiness, but our own, can possibly endanger us, or prevent our receiving Benefit. Doubtless it would both be more pleasing and more edifying, to come to *the Table of the Lord* [a] in Company with such only as are qualified for a Place at it: and they, who are unqualified, ought, when they properly can, to be restrained from it. But we have neither Direction nor Permission to stay away, because others come who should not: nor can they ever be so effectually excluded, but that *Tares* will be mixed *among the Wheat:* and attempting to *root them up* may often be more hurtful than *letting both grow together till the Harvest* [b]. Nay, should even *the Stewards* and Dispensers *of God's Mysteries* [c] be unholy Persons, though it be a grievous Temptation to others to *abhor the Offering*

[a] 1 Cor. x. 21. [b] Matth. xiii. 28—31.
[c] 1 Cor. iv. 2.

of

*of the Lord*ᵈ, yet that is holy still. *They shall bear their Iniquity:* but notwithstanding, *all the Promises* of all God's Ordinances *are yea and Amen,* sure and certain, *in Jesus Christ*ᵉ, to as many as *worship Him in Spirit and in Truth* ᶠ.

ᵈ 1 Sam. ii. 17.   ᵉ 2 Cor. i. 20.   ᶠ John iv. 23.

LECTURE

LECTURE XXXVIII.

Of the LORD'S SUPPER.

PART III.

WHAT Qualifications and Dispositions are *required* of them who come to the Lord's Supper, the Scripture hath not particularly expressed: for they are easily collected from the Nature of this Ordinance. But our Catechism, in its fifth and last Answer concerning it, hath reduced them very justly to three: Repentance, Faith, and Charity.

I. *That we repent us truly of our former Sins, stedfastly proposing to lead a new Life.* For as we are by Nature prone to Sin; and the youngest and best among us have in more Instances than a few been guilty of it: the less the better: so in Christianity,

Repentance

Repentance is the Foundation of every Thing. Now the Sorrow that we ought to feel for the least Sin, must be a very serious one: and for greater Offences in Proportion deeper. But the Vehemence and Paffionateness of Grief will, on every Occafion, and particularly on this, be extremely different in different Perfons. And therefore all, that God expects, is a fincere, though it may be a calm, Concern, for every past Fault, of which we are confcious, and for the Multitudes, which we have either not obferved or forgotten. And this Concern must proceed from a Senfe of Duty, and produce the good Effects of an humble Confeffion to Him in all Cafes, and to our Fellow-Creatures, in all Cafes needful; of Reftitution for the Injuries that we have done, fo far as it is poffible; and of a settled Refolution to amend our Hearts and Lives, wherever it is wanting. More than this we cannot do; and lefs than this God cannot accept. For it would be giving us a Licenfe to difobey Him, if He allowed us to come to his Table, and profefs to *have Fellowship with Him*, while we *walked in Darkness*.

LECTURE XXXVIII.

Darkness[a]. Mere Infirmities indeed, and undesigned Frailties, provided we strive against them with any good Degree of honest Care, and humble ourselves in the Divine Presence for them, so far as we are sensible of them, will not provoke God to reject us, as unworthy Receivers, though in Strictness, we are all unworthy. For if such Failures as these made Persons unfit, nobody could be fit. And therefore they will be no Excuse for omitting what Christ hath commanded: nor can be any Reason why we should not do it with Comfort.

But whoever lives in any wilful Sin, cannot safely come to the holy Sacrament: nor, which I beg you to observe, can he safely stay away. For, as the Hypocrisy of professing Amendment falsely at God's Table is a great Sin; so the Profaneness of turning our Backs upon it, because we will not amend, is to the full as great a one: and it is the merest Folly in the World to chuse either, as the safer Way; for a wicked Person can be safe no Way. But let him resolve to quit his Wickedness: and when

[a] 1 John i. 6.

he is thoroughly sure, so far as he can judge from a competent Experience, that he hath resolved upon it effectually, then he may as safely receive as he can say his Prayers. And such a one should come, not with servile Fear, as to a hard Master; but with willing Duty, as to a merciful Father. Nay, should he afterwards break his Resolutions, though doubtless it would be the justest Cause of heavy Grief, yet it would not prove that he received unworthily, but only that he hath behaved unworthily since he received. And the Thing for him to do is, to lament his Fault with deeper Contrition, renew his good Purposes more firmly, pray for Help from above with more Earnestness, watch over himself with more prudent Care: then go again to God's Altar, thankfully commemorate his pardoning Love, and claim anew the Benefit of his gracious Covenant. Following this Course honestly, he will assuredly gain Ground. And therefore such, as do not gain Ground, do not follow it honestly: but allow themselves to go round in a Circle of sinning, then repenting as they call it, and communicating, then sinning

ning again: as if every Communion did of Courſe wipe off the old Score, and ſo they might begin a new one without Scruple: which is the abſurdeſt, the moſt irreligious, the moſt fatal Imagination, that can be.

II. The next Thing, required of them who come to the Lord's Supper, is *a lively Faith in God's Mercy through Chriſt, with a thankful Remembrance of his Death.* And the Faith neceſſary is a ſettled Perſuaſion, that, for the Sake of the meritorious Obedience and Sufferings of our bleſſed Redeemer, God will pardon true Penitents; together with a comfortable Truſt that we, as ſuch, have an Intereſt in his Merits. But here again you muſt obſerve, that different Perſons may have very different Degrees of this Perſuaſion and Truſt. Some may be *weak in Faith* [b]; may have Cauſe to ſay with Him in the Goſpel of St. *Mark, Lord, I believe; help thou mine Unbelief* [c]; and yet their Prayers, like His, may be graciouſly heard. Others may be *ſtrong* [d], and *increaſe* [e], till they *abound in Faith* [f].

[b] Rom. xiv. 1.   [c] Mark ix. 24.   [d] Rom. iv. 20.
[e] Luke xvii. 5.   [f] Col. ii. 7.

And

And such have great Reason to be thankful to God for themselves: but surely they ought never to judge hardly of their Brethren, who have not advanced so far. The Rule of judging, both in the Catechism and the Scripture, is not by the Positiveness, but the Liveliness, of our Faith; that is, the Fruits of a Christian Life, which it produces: for *Faith without Works is dead* [g]. If we cannot shew the Evidence of these, the highest Confidence will do us no Good: and if we can, we need have no Doubts concerning our spiritual Condition; and though we have ever so many, provided we perceive no sufficient Reason for them, we may celebrate this holy Ordinance very safely. For such Weaknesses in our natural Temper and Spirits are no Way inconsistent with having, in our fixed and deliberate Judgment, that *full Trust in God's Mercy*, which the Communion-Service requires: and we cannot take a more likely Method, either to perfect our Repentance or to strengthen our Faith, than receiving the Sacrament frequently.

[g] Jam. ii. 17.

LECTURE XXXVIII.

Our Catechism teaches further, that our Faith in Christ must be accompanied *with a thankful Remembrance of his Death*. And surely, if we believe, that He died to save us, we must be thankful for it. But then the Measure of our Thankfulness must be taken from the Goodness and Constancy of its Effects, not from that sensible Warmth and Fervency, which we cannot, ordinarily speaking, feel so strongly in spiritual Things as in temporal; and of which bad Persons may at Times have very much, and good Persons little. For that is the true Thankfulness, which produces Love. And *this is the Love of God, that we keep his Commandments*[h].

But there is one Commandment, as I have shewn you, peculiarly connected with this Ordinance. And therefore our Catechism specifies it separately, and in express Terms by requiring,

III. That we *be in Charity with all Men*. For we can have no Share in the Love of our Creator, our Redeemer, and Sanctifier unless, in Imitation of it, we love one an-

[h] 1 John v. 3.

other: and, as the Goodnefs of God is univerfal, fo muſt ours be too. Receiving the holy Communion was indeed intended to increafe the Degree of it: but the Reality we muſt have, before we are worthy to receive. And we muſt ſhew it is real, by *forgiving them who trefpafs againſt us:* by aſſiſting, as far as can be reafonably expected, thofe who need Aſſiſtance in any Kind; by our hearty Prayers for thofe, whom we can help no other Way; by faithfully performing the Duties of our feveral Stations and Relations in Life; and by Condefcention, Mildnefs, and Humanity towards every Perfon, as Occafion offers: all which Duties, and particularly that of Forgivenefs, have been explained to you in their proper Places.

Thefe then being the Difpofitions requifite for receiving the holy Sacrament, as indeed they are for obtaining eternal Happinefs; we are all greatly concerned to examine ourfelves, whether we have them or not: and fhould have been concerned to do it, though this Ordinance had never been appointed. But we are now more efpecially bound to it with a View to this Ordinance;

both

LECTURE XXXVIII.

both from the Nature of it, and from St. *Paul's* positive Injunction: *Let a Man examine himself, and so let him eat of that Bread and drink of that Cup*[i].

The principal Subjects of our Examination are comprehended under the three Heads just now mentioned. But as to any particular Method to be taken, or Time to be spent in it, or in any further Preparation subsequent to it, we have no Command: it is left to every one's Prudence and voluntary Piety. They who live in a constant Practice of Religion and Virtue, are always fit for the Sacrament: and may, if the Call be sudden, by reflecting for a few Moments, sufficiently know that they are fit. Persons, who live in any Sin, may as easily and quickly know that they are not. And it is only in doubtful Cases, that any Length of Consideration is necessary to satisfy us about this Matter. But it must be extremely useful for all Persons, not only to be attentive to their Ways constantly, but to look back upon them frequently; much more frequently than almost any o-

[i] 1 Cor. xi. 28.

the Sacrament. And as Things, which have no certain Seafon fixed for them, are very apt to be neglected; we fhould fix upon this, as one certain Seafon for as particular an Infpection into the State of our Hearts and Lives as we can well make, and can hope to be the better for; joining with it fuitable Meditations, Refolutions, and Devotions. But then in the whole of this Work we muft be careful, neither to hurry over any Part thoughtlefsly, nor lengthen it wearifomely. And in our Examination we muft be efpecially careful, neither to flatter nor yet to affright ourfelves: but obferve impartially, what is right in us thank God, and take the Comfort of it: acknowledge what is wrong, beg Pardon, and amend it. For without Amendment, being ever fo forry will avail nothing.

The laft Thing to be mentioned in Relation to this holy Sacrament, is our Behaviour at it, which ought to be very ferious and reverent; fuch as may fhew, in the propereft Manner, that, to ufe the Apoftle's Words, we *difcern* or diftinguifh *the Lord's Body;*

LECTURE XXXVIII.

Body [k]; look on the Action of receiving it, as one of no common Nature, but as the religious Memorial of our blessed Saviour's dying for us, and by his Death establishing with us a Covenant of Pardon, Grace, and everlasting Felicity, on God's Part, and of Faith and Holiness, on ours. With this important Consideration, we should endeavour to affect our Hearts deeply and tenderly: yet neither to force our Minds, if we could, into immoderate Transports, by which we shall only bewilder and lose, instead of benefiting, ourselves; nor express even what we ought to feel, by any improper Singularities of Gesture; nor yet be dejected, if we have less Feeling, and even less Attention to the Service, than we have Reason to wish. For such Things may be, in a great Measure at least, natural and unavoidable. Or, supposing them Faults; they may be, and often are, the Faults of such Persons, as notwithstanding are, on the whole, very worthy Communicants. They may be, for a Time, useful Means of keeping us humble and watchful: after that, God may deliver us from them;

[k] 1 Cor. xi. 29.

and should we continue all our Lives afflicted with them, it would never hinder our receiving all the necessary Benefits of this Ordinance.

God grant that both it, and all his other gracious Institutions, may contribute effectually to *build us up on our most holy Faith* in a suitable Practice, that so we may ever *keep ourselves in the Love of God*; and on good Grounds *look for the Mercy of our Lord Jesus Christ, unto eternal Life*[1].

[1] Jude. ver. 20, 21.

LECTURE XXXIX.

The Conclusion.

HAVING now, through God's Mercy, carried on thefe Lectures to the End of the Catechifm, and in fome Meafure explained to you every Part of Chriftian Faith and Duty comprehended in it, I have only one Inftruction more to add, but the moft important of all for you to remember and confider well: that, *if ye know thefe Things, happy are ye, if ye do them*[a]; and miferable are ye, if ye do them not.

We all know indeed by Nature, in a great Degree, what Manner of Perfons we ought to be in this World; and therefore, if we fail of being fuch, are in a great Degree inexcufable. For how little Teaching foever fome may have had; yet our Sa-

[a] John, xiii. 17.

viour's home Question will reach even them: *Yea, and why even of yourselves judge ye not, what is right*[b]*? The Work of the Law is written in the Hearts* of Men, *their Conscience also bearing Witness*[c]. Being reasonable Creatures we are evidently bound to govern our Passions, Appetites, Fancies, and whole Behaviour, by the Rules of Reason. And who doth not see, that Sobriety, Temperance and Modesty, are things perfectly reasonable; and Excess, and Dissoluteness, and Indecency, mischievous and shameful? Being social Creatures, we are as evidently bound to whatever will make Society happy. And since we are very sensible, that others ought to treat us with Justice and Kindness, peaceably mind their own Business, and diligently provide for their own Maintenance; we cannot but be sensible, that we ought to do the same Things. Then lastly, being Creatures capable of knowing our Creator, who is *not far from every one of us; for in Him we live, and move, and have our Being*[d]: it follows very clearly, that we are not to forget Him, but worship and obey Him

[b] Luke xii. 57.   [c] Rom. ii. 15.   [d] Acts xvii. 27, 28.

as

LECTURE XXXIX.

as the almighty, all-wife, and all-good Maker and Lord of the Univerſe; acknowledge our Dependance on Him, be thankful to Him for his Mercies, and reſign ourſelves to his Diſpoſal.

Thus much, one ſhould have thought, all Men muſt have known, without ſupernatural Teaching: and certainly they might; and therefore are juſtly blameable and puniſhable, if they do not. But ſtill it hath appeared in Fact, that wherever Men have been left to their own Reaſon, neither every one hath taught himſelf, nor the wiſer Part of the World taught the reſt, even theſe plain Things; ſo as to produce any ſteady Regard to them, as Duties, or even any ſettled Conviction of them, as Truths. And for Want of it, Sin and Miſery have prevailed every where. Men have made others and themſelves wretched in numberleſs Ways: and often doubly wretched by the Reflections of their own Hearts; knowing they had done ill, and not knowing how to be ſure of Pardon.

Foreſeeing from Eternity theſe dreadful Conſequences of human Ignorance and Wickedneſs,

Wickedness, God provided suitable Remedies of Instruction and Grace: which he notified to the World from Time to Time, as his own unsearchable Wisdom saw would be fittest; increasing the Light gradually till it shone out in the full Day of Christianity. But Revelation, as well as Reason, hath been given in vain to a great Part of Mankind. The Propagation of it through the Earth hath been strangely neglected: in many Places, where it hath been received, it hath been lost again: and in too many, where it is retained, it is grievously corrupted and obscured. Without Question we ought to judge as charitably as we can of all who are in any of these Conditions: but at the same Time we ought, from the Bottom of our Hearts, to thank God that none of them is our own. Undoubtedly He is and will be gracious to all his Creatures, as far as they are fit Objects: but it is *the Riches of his Grace*[e], that He hath bestowed on us: and as, with Justice, He might dispose of his own free Gifts as He pleased; so, in Mercy, He hath conferred

[e] Eph. i. 7. ii. 7.

a large

LECTURE XXXIX.

a large Proportion of them on this Nation and Age. Bleſſings, that are common and familiar, though indeed much the greater for that, are uſually but little regarded. And thus, amongſt other Things, the Opportunities that we enjoy of religious Knowledge, it may be feared, are often very lightly eſteemed. But would we reflect, how much leſs Means of being acquainted with the Duties of this Life, and the Rewards of another, not only the unenlightened Heathen World, but the Jews, the People of God, had formerly; and much the greateſt Part even of Chriſtians have had for Numbers of ſucceſſive Generations, and have ſtill, than We: it would make us feel, that our Saviour's Words belong to us alſo: *Verily, I ſay unto you, that many Prophets and righteous Men have deſired to ſee thoſe Things which ye ſee, and have not ſeen them: and to hear thoſe Things which ye hear, and have not heard them. But bleſſed are your Eyes, for they ſee; and your Ears, for they hear* [f].

But then, and, for the Sake of God and our Souls, let us obſerve it; if *ſeeing we ſee*

[f] Matth. xiii. 16, 17.

not, and hearing we hear not [g], to the only good Purpose of Life, that of becoming in Heart and in Practice such as we ought; *better had it been for us, not to have known the Way of Righteousness, than, after we have known it, to turn from the holy Commandment delivered unto us* [h]. *For unto whomsoever much is given, of him shall much be required. The Servant, that knew his Lord's Will, and prepared not himself, neither did according to his Will, shall be beaten with many Stripes: he that knew it not with few* [i]. But take Notice; he that, in Comparison with others, may be said not to know the Will of God, knows enough of it however to subject him if he fails of doing it, to future Punishment; *to be beaten with Stripes.* Not even a heathen Sinner therefore shall escape intirely by his Ignorance: much less will that Plea excuse a Christian; but least of all can those Christians hope for Mercy, who hear the Word of God preached to them weekly; have it in their Hands, and may read it daily; and yet transgress it. *Verily I say unto you, it shall be more tolerable for Sodom*

[g] Matth. xiii. 13.   [h] 2 Pet. ii. 21.   [i] Luke xii. 47, 48.

and

LECTURE XXXIX.

and Gomorrha, in the Day of Judgment [k], than for such Persons.

Let no one argue from hence, that Knowledge then is no Blessing. For the more we know of our Maker and our Duty, the better we are qualified to be good in this World, and happy in the next. And we can never be worse for it, unless we will, by making either no Use or a bad Use of it. Nor let any one imagine, that, though we need not be the worse for our Knowledge, yet since we may, Ignorance is the safer Choice; as what will excuse our Sins, if not intirely, yet in a great Measure. But let us all remember, it is not pretended, but real; Ignorance; nor even that, unless we could not help it, that will be any Plea in our Favour. Wilful, or even careless Ignorance, is a great Sin itself; and therefore can never procure us Pardon for the other Sins which it may occasion. What should any of us think of a Servant who kept out of the Way of receiving his Master's Orders, purposely because he had no Mind to do them? Nay, supposing him

[k] Mark vi. 11.

only

LECTURE XXXIX.

only through Negligence not to underſtand the Buſineſs that he was required to learn and follow: would this juſtify him? Would it not be ſaid, that what he might and ought to have known, it was his own Fault if he did not know? And what do we think of God, if we hope to impoſe on Him with Pleas that will not paſs amongſt ourſelves?

Fix it in your Hearts then: the firſt indiſpenſable Duty of Man is, to learn the Will of his Maker; the next to do it: and nothing can excuſe you from either. Attend therefore diligently on all ſuch Means of Inſtruction, as God's Providence gives you: eſpecially the publick Inſtruction of the Church, which, having expreſsly appointed for you, he will aſſuredly bleſs to you; provided you obſerve our Saviour's moſt important Direction, *Take heed how you hear*[l]. For on that it depends, whether the preaching of the Goſpel ſhall be *Life or Death to you*[m]. One it muſt be: and theſe very Lectures, amongſt other Things, which have been truly intended for your eternal

[l] Luke viii. 18.   [m] 2 Cor. ii. 16.

Good,

LECTURE XXXIX.

Good, will prove, if you apply them not to that End, what God forbid they should, a Means of increasing your future Condemnation. Be intreated therefore to consider very seriously what you are taught; for be there ever so much of the Weakness of Man in it, there is the Power of God unto Salvation, unless you hinder it yourselves. Never despise then the meanest of your Instructors; and never think of admiring the ablest: but remember that your Business is, neither to applaud nor censure other Persons Performances; but to improve your own Hearts, and mend your own Lives. Barely coming and hearing is nothing. Barely being pleased and moved and affected is nothing. It is only minding and doing the whole of your Duty, not some Part of it alone, that is any Thing.

Knowing the Words of your Catechism is of no other Use, than to preserve in your Memories the Things which those Words express. Knowing the Meaning of your Catechism ever so well, in every Part, is of no other Use than to put you on the Performance of what it teaches. And performing

forming some Things ever so constantly or zealously, will not avail, without a faithful Endeavour to perform every Thing. Have it always in your Thoughts therefore, that Practice, uniform Practice, is the one Thing needful. Your Knowledge may be very low and Imperfect, your Faith not very clear and distinct: but however poorly you are capable of furnishing your Heads; if your Hearts and Lives be good, all is well.

But here, I pray you, observe further, that as it is not in understanding and believing, so it is not in Devotion merely, that Religion consists. The common Duties of common Life make far the greatest Part of what our Maker expects of us. To be honest and sober, and modest and humble, and good-tempered and mild, and industrious and useful in our several Stations, are Things to which all Persons are as much bound as they can be to any Thing: and when they proceed from a Principle of Conscience towards God, and are offered up to Him, as our bounden Duty, through Jesus Christ; are as true and as acceptable a Service to Him, as either our Attendance at Church,

or

or our Prayers in Retirement at Home. And they, who abound in thefe latter Duties, and neglect any of the former, only difgrace Religion, and deceive themfelves.

Yet underftand me, I beg you not to fpeak flightly of Devotion, either private or publick. On the contrary, I recommend both to you moft earneftly: for our immediate Duty to God is the higheft of all Duties, *the firft and great Commandment*[n] of natural Religion: and the Payment of due and diftinct Regards to the Father almighty, to his bleffed Son, and holy Spirit, of Courfe obtains an equal Rank in Revelation. In particular I recommend it to you not to omit coming to Evening-Prayers, becaufe now thefe Lectures will be difcontinued. Joining in God's Worfhip, and hearing his holy Word read to you, is always a fufficient, and fhould always be the principal, Motive to bring you. For *neither is he that planteth, any Thing; neither he that watereth: but God, that giveth the Increafe*[o]. And we may be fure He will give it to

---

[n] Matth. xxii. 38.   [o] 1 Cor. iii. 7.

those, who attend on his Ordinances with pious Minds: and we may juftly expect, that He will withhold it from thofe who, inftead of coming becaufe it is their Duty, come to hear this or that Man difcourfe.

But then I muft befeech you to obferve at the fame Time; that as neither Piety without Morals, nor Morals without Piety, nor heathen Piety without Chriftian, will fuffice; fo neither will the outward Acts of any Thing, without an inward Principle of it; and the true Principle is a reverent Efteem and Love of God. Other Inducements may allowably be joined with this: but if this be not alfo joined with them, what we do may be Prudence, may be Virtue, but is not Religion; and therefore, however right, fo far as it goes, doth not go far enough to intitle us to Reward, or even to fecure us from Punifhment; which nothing can more juftly deferve, than to have little or no Senfe of filial Affection to our heavenly Father, and of thankful Love to our crucified Redeemer and gracious Sanctifier, who have the higheft Right to the utmoft Regard that our Souls are capable of feeling.

You

LECTURE XXXIX.

You muſt reſolve therefore, not only to be Chriſtians externally in your Lives, but internally in your Hearts. And, let me remind you further, you will reſolve on neither to good Purpoſe, if you truſt to yourſelves alone for the Performance. You will contrive, perhaps, great Schemes of Amendment and Goodneſs; but you will execute very little of them: or you will do a good deal, it may be, in ſome Particulars; and leave others, equally neceſſary, undone: or you will go on a while; and then fall when you thought you were fureſt of ſtanding: or what ſeeming Progreſs ſoever you make, you will ruin it all, by thinking too highly of yourſelves for it: or ſome Way or another you will certainly fail; unleſs the Grace of God enable you, firſt to be deeply ſenſible of your own Guilt and Weakneſs; then to lay hold, by Faith in Chriſt, on his promiſed Mercy and Help; in the Strength of that Help to obey his Commands; and after all to know, that you are ſtill *unprofitable Servants*?. Now this Grace you may certainly have, in whatever Mea-

? Luke xvii. 10.

sure you want it, by earnest Prayer for it, humble Dependance upon it, and such honest and diligent Use of the lower Degrees of it, as He hath promised to reward with higher Degrees: and you can have it no other Way. If ever therefore, when we exhort you to Duties, moral or religious, we omit to mention the great Duty of applying for Strength from above to be given you, not for your own Sakes, but that of your blessed Redeemer, in order to practise them: it is by no Means because we think such Application unnecessary; but because we hope you know it so well to be absolutely necessary, that we need not always remind you of it. But if we are, at any Time, wanting to you in this Respect, or any other; be not you therefore wanting to yourselves; *but work out your own Salvation* from this Motive, which alone will procure you Success, that *God worketh in you both to will and to do* [q]. *And I pray God to sanctify you wholly, and preserve your whole Spirit, Soul, and Body, blameless, unto the Coming of our Lord Jesus Christ* [r].

[q] Phil. ii. 12, 13. [r] 1 Thess. v. 23.

Having

LECTURE XXXIX.

Having said thus much to you all in general, I desire you, Children, to take Notice of what I am going to say, in the last Place, to you in particular. Your Condition is of the lower Kind: but your Instruction hath been better than many of your Superiors have had. If therefore your Behaviour be bad, your Condemnation will be heavy; and if it be good, you may be to the full as happy, in this World and the next, as if you were of ever so high Rank. For true Happiness comes only from doing our Duty; and none will ever come from transgressing it: but, whatever Pleasure or Profit Sin may promise, they will soon turn into Pain and Loss. Remember therefore, as long as you live, what you have been taught here. Remember particularly the Answers to those two main Questions: *What is thy Duty towards God*; and, *What is thy Duty towards thy Neighbour*. And be assured, that unless you practise both, when you go hence to Services and Apprenticeships, all the Money and Labour, that hath been spent on you, will be spent in vain; you will be a Disgrace to the Education and Teaching that you have had;

you will probably be very miserable here, and certainly so for ever hereafter. But, if you practise both, you will make an honest and grateful Return for the Kindness that you have received from your Benefactors; which I hope you will never forget, but imitate, if God enable you to do it: you will be loved of your Maker and Fellow-Creatures; you will live in Peace of Mind, you will die with Comfort, and be received into everlasting Bliss.

Think then, I entreat and charge you, seriously and often of these Things. And to remind yourselves of them more effectually, be diligent in reading such good Books as are given you at your leaving School, or otherwise put into your Hands: be constant in coming to Church, on the Lord's Days at least: such of you, as go away before you are confirmed, take the first Opportunity, after you are fourteen, to apply to your Minister wherever you are, that you may be well instructed for that holy Ordinance, and then admitted to it. Within a reasonable Time after this, prepare yourselves, and desire him and your Friends to assist in preparing

ing you, to receive the Lord's Supper: concerning which you have heard very lately, how exprefsly it is required of all Chriftians, (a Name that comprehends young as well as old) for the Means of improving them in every Thing that is good. And may God give his Grace to you and to us all, that by the Help of thofe Means, with which He hath fo plentifully favoured us, we may each of us improve daily in the Knowledge of his Truth, and the Love of our Duty, *till at length we come unto a perfect Man, unto the Meafure of the Stature of the Fulnefs of Chrift*[s].

[s] Eph. iv. 13.

A SERMON

A SERMON ON CONFIRMATION.

Acts viii. 17.

Then laid they their Hands on them, and they received the Holy Ghoſt.

THE Hiſtory, to which theſe Words belong, is this. *Philip* the Deacon, ordained at the ſame Time with St. *Stephen,* had converted and baptized the People of *Samaria:* which the Apoſtles at *Jeruſalem* hearing, ſent down to them *Peter* and *John,* two of their own Body; who by Prayer, accompanied with Impoſition of Hands, obtained for them a greater Degree, than they had yet received, of the ſacred Influences of the Divine Spirit: which undoubtedly was done on their ſignifying in ſome Manner, ſo as to be underſtood, their Adherence to the Engagement, into which they had entered at their Baptiſm.

From this and the like Inſtances of the Practice of the Apoſtles, is derived, what
Biſhops

Bishops, their Successors, though every Way beyond Comparison inferior to them, have practised ever since, and which we now call Confirmation. Preaching was common to all Ranks of Ministers: baptizing was performed usually by the lower Rank: but perhaps to maintain a due Subordination, it was reserved to the highest, by Prayer and laying on of Hands, to communicate further Measures of the Holy Ghost. It was indeed peculiar to the Apostles, that on their Intercession, his extraordinary and miraculous Gifts were bestowed: which continued in the Church no longer, than the Need of them did; nor can we suppose, that all were Partakers of them. But unquestionably by their Petitions they procured, for every sincere Convert, a much more valuable, though less remarkable Blessing, of universal and perpetual Necessity, his ordinary and saving Graces.

For these therefore, after their Example, trusting that God will have Regard, not to our Unworthiness, but to the Purposes of Mercy which He hath appointed us to serve, we interceed now, when Persons

take

take upon themselves the Vow of their Baptism. For this good End being now come amongst you, though I doubt not but your Ministers have given you proper Instructions on the Occasion: yet I am desirous of adding somewhat further, which may not only acquaint more fully those, who are especially concerned, with the Nature of what they are about to do, but remind you all of the Obligations, which Christianity lays upon you. And I cannot perform it better, than by explaining to you the Office of Confirmation, to which you may turn in your Prayer Books, where it stands immediately after the Catechism.

There you will see, in the first Place, a Preface, directed to be read: in which, Notice is given, that *for the more edifying of such as shall receive Confirmation*, it shall be administered to none but those, *who can answer to the Questions of the Catechism* preceding: that so *Children* may *come to Years of* some *Discretion*, and *learn what* the *Promise* made for them *in Baptism* was, before they are called upon to *ratify and confirm it before the Church with their own Consent*,

and

and to engage *that they will evermore observe it*.

Prayers may be offered up for Infants with very good Effect. Promises may be made in their Name by such as are authorised to act for them: especially when the Things promised are for their Interest, and will be their Duty; which is the Case of those in Baptism. But no Persons ought to make Promises for themselves, till they reasonably well understand the Nature of them, and are capable of forming serious Purposes. Therefore, in the present Case, being able to say the Words of their Catechism is by no Means enough, without a competent general Knowledge of their Meaning, and Intention of behaving as it requires them; which doubtless they are supposed to have at the same Time. And if they have not; making a Profession of it, is declaring with their Mouths what they feel not in their Hearts at the Instant, and will much less reflect upon afterwards: it is hoping to please God by the empty outward Performance of a religious Rite, from which if they had been withheld, till they

they were duly qualified, their Souls might have been affected, and their Conduct influenced by it, as long as they lived.

Therefore I hope and beg, that neither Ministers nor Parents will be too eager for bringing Children very early to Confirmation: but first teach them carefully, to know their Duty sufficiently, and resolve upon the Practice of it heartily; then introduce them to this Ordinance: which they shall not fail to have Opportunities of attending in their Neighbourhood, from Time to Time, so long as God continues my Life and Strength.

But as there are some too young for Confirmation, some also may be thought too old: especially, if they have received the holy Sacrament without it. Now there are not indeed all the same Reasons for the Confirmation of such, as of others: nor hath the Church, I believe, determined any Thing about their Case, as it might be thought unlikely to happen. But still, since it doth happen too frequently, that Persons were not able, or have neglected, to apply for this Purpose: so whenever they apply,

as

as by doing it they exprefs a Defire to *fulfill all Righteoufnefs*[a]; and may certainly receive Benefit, both from the Profeffion and the Prayers, appointed in the Office: my Judgment is, that they fhould not be rejected, but encouraged.

Only I muft intreat you to obferve, that when you take thus on yourfelves the Engagement of leading a Chriftian Life, you are to take it once for all; and no more to think of ever being confirmed a fecond Time, than of being baptized a fecond Time.

After directing, Who are to be confirmed; the Office goes on to direct, How they are to be confirmed. And here, the Bifhop is to begin with afking every one of thofe, who offer themfelves, whether they *do, in the Prefence of God and of the Congregation, renew in their own Perfons the folemn Vow of their Baptifm; acknowledging themfelves bound to believe and to perform all thofe Things, which their God-Fathers and God-Mothers then undertook for them.* On which

---

[a] Matth. iii. 15.

they are each of them to anſwer, with an audible Voice, *I do.*

Now the Things, promiſed in our Name, were, to renounce whatever God hath forbidden, to believe what He hath taught, and to practiſe what He hath commanded. Nobody can promiſe for Infants abſolutely, that they ſhall do theſe Things; but only, that they ſhall be inſtructed and admoniſhed to do them: and, it is hoped, not in vain. This Inſtruction and Admonition, Parents are obliged by Nature to give; and if they do it effectually, God-Fathers and God-Mothers have no further Concern, than to be heartily glad of it. But if the former fail, the latter muſt ſupply the Failure, as far as they have Opportunity of doing it with any reaſonable Proſpect of Succeſs. For they were intended, not to releaſe the Parents from the Care of their Children, which nothing can: but for a double Security, in a Caſe of ſuch Importance.

If nothing at all had been promiſed in our Names, we had ſtill been bound, as ſoon as we were capable of it, to believe in God, and obey Him. But we are more early

early and more firmly bound, as not only this hath been promised for us, but Care hath been taken to make us sensible of our Obligation to perform it: which Obligation therefore, Persons are called upon, in the Question under Consideration, to ratify and confirm. And great Cause have they to answer, that they do. For doing it is a Duty, on which their eternal Felicity peculiarly depends: as a little Attention to what I am about to say will clearly shew you.

Our first Parents, even while they were innocent, had no Title to Happiness, or to Existence, but from God's Notification of his good Pleasure: which being conditional, when they fell, they lost it; and derived to Us a corrupt and mortal Nature, intitled to nothing; as both the Diseases and the Poverty of Ancestors often descend to their distant Posterity. This bad Condition we fail not, from our first Use of Reason, to make worse, in a greater or less Degree, by actual Transgressions: and so personally deserve the Displeasure, instead of Favour, of Him, who made us. Yet

we

CONFIRMATION.

we may hope, that as He is good, He will on our Repentance forgive us. But then, as He is also just and wise, and the Ruler of the World; we could never know with Certainty, of ourselves, what his Justice and Wisdom and the Honour of his Government might require of Him with Respect to Sinners: whether He would pardon great Offences at all; and whether He would reward those, whom He might be pleased not to punish. But most happily the Revelation of his holy Word hath cleared up all these Doubts of unassisted Reason: and offered to the worst of Sinners, on the Condition of Faith in Christ, added to Repentance, and productive of good Works (for all which He is ready to enable us,) a Covenant of Pardon for Sins past, Assistance against Sin for the future, and eternal Life in return for a sincere, though imperfect, and totally undeserving, Obedience.

The Method of entering into this Covenant is, being baptized in the Name of the Father, the Son, and the Holy Ghost: that is, into the Acknowledgment of the

U 2   mysterious

mysterious Union and joint Authority of these Three; and of the distinct Offices, which they have undertaken for our Salvation: together with a faithful Engagement of paying suitable Regard to each of them. In this Appointment of Baptism, the washing with Water aptly signifies, both our Promise to preserve ourselves, with the best Care we can, pure from the Defilement of Sin, and God's Promise to consider us, as free from the Guilt of it. Baptism then, through his Mercy, secures Infants from the bad Consequences of *Adam*'s Transgression, giving them a new Title to the Immortality, which he lost. It also secures, to Persons grown up, the intire Forgiveness of their own Transgressions, on the Terms just mentioned. But then, in order to receive these Benefits, we must lay our Claim to the Covenant, which conveys them: we must ratify, as soon as we are able, what was promised in our Name by others before we were able; and done for us then, only on Presumption that we would make it our own Deed afterwards. For if we neglect, and appear to renounce our Part of the Covenant, we have plainly not the least Right to God's performing His: but we remain in our Sins, and *Christ shall profit us nothing* [b].

You see then of what unspeakable Importance it is, that we take on ourselves the Vow of our Baptism. And it is very fit and useful, that we should take it in such Form and Manner as the Office prescribes. It is fit, that when Persons have been properly instructed by the Care of their Parents, Friends, and Ministers, they should with joyful Gratitude acknowledge them to have faithfully performed that kindest Duty. It is fit, that before they are admitted by the Church of Christ to the holy Communion, they should give public Assurance to the Church of their Christian Belief and Christian Purposes. This may also be extremely useful to themselves. For consider: young Persons are just entering into a World full of Temptations, with no Experience, and little Knowledge to guard them; and much youthful Rashness, to expose them. The Authority of other

[b] Gal. v. 2.

over

over them is beginning to lessen, their own Passions to increase, *evil Communication* to have great Opportunities of *corrupting good Manners*[c]: and strong Impressions, of one Kind or another, will be made on them very soon. What can then be more necessary, or more likely to preserve their Innocence, than to form the most deliberate Resolutions of acting right; and to declare them in a Manner, thus adapted to move them at the Time, and be remembered by them afterwards: in the Presence of God, of a Number of his Ministers, and of a large Congregation of his People, assembled with more than ordinary Solemnity for that very Purpose?

But then you, that are to be confirmed, must either do your own Part, or the whole of this Preparation will be utterly thrown away upon you. If you make the Answer, which is directed, without Sincerity, it is lying to God: if you make it without Attention, it is trifling with him. Watch over your Hearts therefore, and let them go along with your Lips. The two short

[c] 1 Cor. xv. 33.

Words,

Words, *I do*, are soon said: but they comprehend much in them. Whoever uses them on this Occasion, saith in Effect as follows. " *I do* heartily renounce all the
" Temptations of the Devil; all the un-
" lawful Pleasures, Profits, and Honours
" of the World; all the immoral Gratifica-
" tions of the Flesh. *I do* sincerely believe,
" and will constantly profess, all the Arti-
" cles of the Christian Faith. *I do* firmly
" resolve to keep all God's Commandments
" all the Days of my Life; to love and
" honour Him; to pray to Him, and praise
" Him daily in private; to attend con-
" scientiously on the public Worship and
" Instruction, which He hath appointed;
" to approach his holy Table, as soon as
" I can qualify myself for doing it worthi-
" ly; to submit to his blessed Will meekly
" and patiently in all Things; to set Him
" ever before my Eyes, and acknowledge
" Him in all my Ways. *I do* further re-
" solve, in the whole Course of my Be-
" haviour amongst my Fellow-Creatures,
" to *do justly, love Mercy*[d], speak Truth,

[d] Mic. vi. 8.

"be diligent and useful in my Station,
"dutiful to my Superiors, condescending
"to those beneath me, friendly to my
"Equals; careful, through all the Rela-
"tions of Life, to act as the Nature of
"them requires, and conduct myself so to
"all Men, as I should think it reasonable
"that they should to me in the like Case.
"Further yet: *I do* resolve, in the Govern-
"ment of myself, to be modest, sober,
"temperate, mild, humble, contented; to
"restrain every Passion and Appetite within
"due Bounds; and to set my heart chiefly,
"not on the sensual Enjoyments of this
"transitory World, but the spiritual Hap-
"piness of the future endless one. Lastly,
"*I do* resolve, whenever I fail in any of
"these Duties, as I am sensible I have,
"and must fear I shall, to confess it before
"God with unfeigned Concern, to apply
"for his promised Pardon in the Name
"of his blessed Son, to beg the promised
"Assistance of his holy Spirit; and in that
"Strength, not my own, to strive against
"my Faults, and watch over my Steps with
"redoubled Care."

Observe

CONFIRMATION. 313

Observe then: it is not Gloominess and Melancholy, that Religion calls you to: it is not useless Austerity, and Abstinence from Things lawful and safe: it is not extravagant Flights and Raptures: it is not unmeaning or unedifying Forms and Ceremonies: much less is it Bitterness against those who differ from you. But the forementioned unquestionable substantial Duties are the Things to which you bind yourselves, when you pronounce the awful Words, *I do*. Utter them then with the truest Seriousness: and say to yourselves, each of you, afterwards, as *Moses* did to the *Jews*, *Thou hast avouched the Lord this Day to be thy God, to walk in his Ways and keep his Statutes, and to hearken to his Voice: and the Lord hath avouched thee this Day to be His; that thou shouldest keep all his Commandments, and be holy unto the Lord thy God, as He hath spoken*[e]. It is a certain Truth, call it therefore often to Mind, and fix it in your Souls, that if breaking a solemn Promise to Men be a Sin; breaking that which you make thus deliberately to God, would be unspeakably a greater Sin.

[e] Deut. xxvi. 17, 18, 19.

But

But let us now proceed to the next Part of the Office: in which, after Persons have confirmed and ratified the Vow of their Baptism, Prayers are offered up, that God would confirm and strengthen them in their good Purpose: on both which Accounts this Appointment is called Confirmation.

Scripture teaches, and sad Experience proves, that of *ourselves we can do nothing*; *are not sufficient* [f] for the Discharge of our Duty, without God's continual Aid: by which He can certainly influence our Minds without hurting our natural Freedom of Will, and even without our perceiving it: for we can influence our Fellow Creatures so. Nor is it any Injustice in Him to require of us what exceeds our Ability, since He is ready to supply the Want of it. Indeed, on the contrary, as this Method of treating us is excellently fitted both to keep us humble, and yet to give us Courage, using it is evidently worthy of God. But then, as none can have Reason to expect his Help, but those who earnestly desire it, so He hath promised to *give*

---

[f] John xv. 5. 2 Cor. iii. 5.

the holy Spirit only *to them that aſk Him* [g]. And to unite Chriſtians more in Love to each other, and incline them more to aſſemble for public Worſhip, our bleſſed Redeemer hath eſpecially promiſed, that *where two or three* of them *are gathered together in his Name, He will be in the Midſt of them* [h]. And further ſtill, to promote a due Regard in his People to their Teachers and Rulers, the ſacred Writings aſcribe a peculiar Efficacy to their praying over thoſe who are committed to their Charge. Even under the Jewiſh Diſpenſation, the Family of *Aaron* were told, that *them the Lord had ſeparated to miniſter unto Him, and to bleſs in the Name of the Lord* [i]: *and they ſhall put my Name,* faith God, *upon the Children of Iſrael, and I will bleſs them* [k] No Wonder then, if under the Chriſtian Diſpenſation we read, but juſt before the Text, that the Apoſtles, *when they were come down to* Samaria, *prayed for* the new-baptized Converts, *that they might receive the Holy Ghoſt*; and in the Text, that they did receive it accordingly.

[g] Luke xi. 13. xxi. 5.   [h] Matth. xviii. 20.   [i] Deut. x. 8.
[k] Num. vi. 27.

Therefore,

Therefore, pursuant to these great Authorities, here is, on the present Occasion, a Number of young Disciples, about to run the same common Race, met together to pray for themselves and one another: here is a Number of elder Christians, who have experienced the Dangers of Life, met to pray for those who are just entering into them: here are also God's Ministers, purposely come, to intercede with Him in their Behalf: and surely we may hope, their joint and fervent Petitions will avail, and be effectual.

They begin, as they ought, with acknowledging, and in Scripture Words, that *our Help is in the Name of the Lord, who hath made Heaven and Earth*[l]: *it is not in Man to direct his own Steps*[m], but his Creator only can preserve him. Then we go on to pronounce *the Name of the Lord blessed, henceforth World without End*, for his Readiness to bestow on us the Grace which we want. And lastly, in Confidence of his Goodness, we intreat Him to *hear our Prayers, and let our Cry come unto Him*[n].

[l] Pf. cxxiv. 8.   [m] Jer. x. 23.   [n] Pf. cii. 1.

After

CONFIRMATION. 317

After thefe preparatory Ejaculations, and the ufual Admonition to be attentive, *Let us pray*; comes a longer Act of Devotion, which firft commemorates God's Mercy already beftowed, then petitions for an Increafe of it. The Commemoration fets forth, that He *hath regenerated thefe his Servants by Water and the Holy Ghoft:* that is, intitled them by Baptifm to the enlivening Influences of the Spirit, and fo, as it were, begotten them again into a State, inexpreffibly happier than their natural one; a Covenant-State, in which God will confider them, whilft they keep their Engagements, with peculiar Love, as his dear Children. It follows, that He *hath given unto them Forgivenefs of all their Sins*; meaning, that He hath given them Affurance of it, on the gracious Terms of the Gofpel. But that every one of them hath actually received it, by complying with thofe Terms fince he finned laft, though we may charitably hope, we cannot prefume to affirm: nor were thefe Words intended to affirm it; as the known Doctrine of the Church of *England* fully proves.

And

And therefore let no one misunderstand this Expression in the Office, which hath parallel ones in the New Testament [o], so as either to censure it, or delude himself with a fatal Imagination, that any Thing said over him can possibly convey to him a Pardon of Sins, for which he is not truly penitent. We only acknowledge, with due Thankfulness, that God hath done his Part: but which of the Congregation have done theirs, their own Consciences must tell them.

After this Commemoration, we go on to request for the Persons before us, that God would *strengthen them* against all Temptation, and support them under all Affliction, by *the Holy Ghost the Comforter, and daily increase in them his manifold Gifts of Grace:* which Gifts we proceed to enumerate in seven Particulars, taken from the Prophet *Isaiah* [p]; by whom they are ascribed to our blessed Redeemer: but as *the same Mind* ought to *be in us, which was in Christ Jesus* [q], a Petition for them was

[o] Eph. i. 7. Col. i. 14.   [p] Isa. xi. 2.
[q] Phil. ii. 5.

used,

CONFIRMATION.   319

used, in the Office of Confirmation, 1400 Years ago, if not sooner. The separate Meaning of each of the seven, it is neither easy nor needful to determine with Certainty. For indeed, if no more was designed, than to express very fully and strongly, by various Words of nearly the same Import, a pious and moral Temper of Mind: this is a Manner of speaking both common and emphatical. But each of them may be taken in a distinct Sense of its own. And thus we may beg for these our Fellow-Christians, a *Spirit of Wisdom*, to aim at the right End, the Salvation of their Souls: and *of Understanding*, to pursue it by right Means: *of Counsel*, to form good Purposes; and of *ghostly* or spiritual *Strength*, to execute them: *of* useful *Knowledge* in the Doctrines of Religion; *and true Godliness*, disposing them to a proper Use of it. But chiefly, though lastly, we pray, that they may be *filled with the Spirit of God's holy Fear:* with that Reverence of Him, as the greatest and purest and best of Beings, the rightful Proprietor and just Judge of all, which will effectually excite

them

them to whatever they are concerned to believe or do. For *the Fear of the Lord is the Beginning of Wisdom*[r].

Having concluded this Prayer for them all in general, the Bishop implores the Divine Protection and Grace for each one, or each Pair of them, in particular: that as he is already God's professed *Child* and *Servant*, by the Recognition which he hath just made of his baptismal Covenant, *so he may continue his for ever*, by faithfully keeping it: *and*, far from decaying, *daily increase in his holy Spirit*, that is, in the Fruits of the Spirit, Piety and Virtue, *more and more*; making greater and quicker Advances in them, as Life goes on, *until he come to* that decisive Hour, when his Portion shall be unchangeable in *God's everlasting Kingdom*.

And, along with the Utterance of these solemn Words, he lays his Hand on each of their Heads: a Ceremony used from the earliest Ages by religious Persons, when they prayed for God's Blessing on any one; used by our Saviour, who, when *Children*

[r] Pf. cxi. 10.

were

were *brought to Him, that He should put his Hands on them, and pray, and bless them, was much displeased*[s] with those who forbad it; used by the Apostles, after Converts were baptized, as the Text plainly shews; reckoned in the Epistle to the *Hebrews* among *the Foundations* of the Christian Profession [t]; constantly practised, and highly esteemed in the Church from that Time to this; and so far from being a popish Ceremony, that the Papists administer Confirmation by other Ceremonies of their own devising, and have laid aside this primitive one; which therefore our Church very prudently restored. And the Custom of it is approved, as apostolical, both by *Luther* and *Calvin,* and several of their Followers, though they rashly abolished it, as having been abused[u]. But I am credibly informed, that at *Geneva* it hath lately been restored.

The laying on of the Hand naturally expresses good Will and good Wishes in the

---

[s] Matth. xix. 13—15. Mark x. 13—16. [t] Heb. vi. 1.
[u] See Camfield's two Discourses on Episcopal Confirmation. 8vo. 1682. p. 23—36.

Person who doth it: and in the present Case is further intended, as you will find in one of the following Prayers, to *certify those,* to whom it is done, *of God's Favour and gracious Goodness towards them:* of which Goodness they will certainly feel the Effects, provided, which must always be understood, that they preserve their Title to his Care by a proper Care of themselves. This, it must be owned, is a Truth: and we may as innocently signify it by this Sign as by any other, or as by any Words to the same Purpose. Further Efficacy we do not ascribe to it: nor would have you look on Bishops, as having or claiming a Power, in any Case, to confer Blessings arbitrarily on whom they please; but only as petitioning God for that Blessing from above which He alone can give; yet, we justly hope, will give the rather for the Prayers of those whom He hath placed over his People, unless your own Unworthiness prove an Impediment. Not that you are to expect, on the Performance of this good Office, any sudden and sensible Change in your Hearts, giving you, all at once, a remarkable

able Strength or Comfort in Piety, which you never felt before. But you may reasonably promise yourselves, from going through it with a proper Disposition, greater Measures, when real Occasion requires them, of such Divine Assistance as will be needful for your Support and orderly Growth in every Virtue of a Christian Life.

And now, the Imposition of Hands being finished, the Bishop and Congregation mutually recommend each other to God, and return to such joint and public Devotions as are suitable to the Solemnity. The first of these is the Lord's Prayer: a Form seasonable always, but peculiarly now; as every Petition in it will shew to every one who considers it. In the next Place, more especial Supplications are poured forth, for the Persons particularly concerned, to Him, who alone can enable them *both to will and to do* what is *good*; that, as the Hand of his Minister hath been laid upon them, so *His fatherly Hand may ever be over them, and lead them in* the only Way, *the Knowledge and Obedience of his Word*, to everlast-

ing Life. After this, a more general Prayer is offered up for them and the rest of the Congregation together, that God would *vouchsafe,* unworthy as we all are, so *to direct and govern both our Hearts and Bodies,* our Inclinations and Actions, (for neither will suffice without the other) *in the Ways of his Laws, and in the Works of his Commandments,* that, *through his most mighty Protection, both here and ever, we may be preserved in Body and Soul:* having the former, in his good Time, raised up from the Dead, and the latter made happy, in Conjunction with it, to all Eternity.

These Requests being thus made, it only remains, that all be dismissed with a solemn Blessing: which will certainly abide with you, unless, by wilful Sin or gross Negligence, you drive it away. And in that Case, you must not hope, that your Baptism, or your Confirmation, or the Prayers of the Bishop, or the Church, or the whole World, will do you any Service. On the contrary, every Thing which you might have been the better for, if you had made a good Use of it, you will be the worse

worse for, if you make a bad one. You do well to renew the Covenant of your Baptism in Confirmation: but, if you break it, you forfeit the Benefit of it. You do well to repeat your Vows in the Sacrament of the Lord's Supper: it is what all Christians are commanded to do by their dying Saviour, *for the strengthening and refreshing of their Souls:* it is what I beg all, who are confirmed, will remember, and their Friends and Ministers remind them of: the sooner they are prepared for it, the happier; and by stopping short, the Benefit of what preceded will be lost. But if you are admitted to this Privilege also, and live wickedly, you do but *eat and drink your own Condemnation.* So that all depends on a thoroughly honest Care of your Hearts and Behaviour in all Respects.

Not that, with our best Care, we can avoid smaller Faults. And if we intreat Pardon for them in our daily Prayers, and faithfully strive against them, they will not be imputed to us. But gross and habitual Sins we may avoid, through God's Help: and if we fall into them, we fall from our

Title to Salvation at the same Time. Yet even then our Case is not desperate: and let us not make it so, by thinking it is: for, through the Grace of the Gospel, we may still repent and amend, and then be forgiven. But I beg you to observe, that, as continued Health is vastly preferable to the happiest Recovery from Sickness; so is Innocence to the truest Repentance. If we suffer ourselves to transgress our Duty; God knows whether we shall have Time to repent: God knows whether we shall have a Heart to do it. At best we shall have lost, and more than lost, the whole Time that we have been going back: whereas we have all Need to press forwards, as fast as we can. Therefore let the innocent of wilful Sin preserve themselves so with the greatest Circumspection; and the Faulty return from their Errors without Delay. Let the Young enter upon the Way of Righteousness with hearty Resolution; and those of riper Age persevere in it to the End. In a Word, let us all, of every Age, seriously consider, and faithfully practise, the Obligations of Religion.

For

For *the Vows of God are* still *upon us* [w], how long soever it be since they were first made, either by us, or for us: and it is in vain to forget what He will assuredly remember; or hope to be safe in neglecting what He expects us to do. But let us use proper Diligence; and He will infallibly give us proper Assistance, and *confirm us* all *unto the End, that we may be blameless in the Day of our Lord Jesus Christ* [x].

Now unto Him, who is able to keep us from falling, and to present us faultless before the Presence of his Glory with exceeding Joy, to the only wise God, our Saviour, be Glory and Majesty, Dominion and Power, both now and ever. Amen [y].

[w] Pf. lvi. 12.   [x] 1 Cor. i. 8.   [y] Jude 24, 25.

THE END.

www.ingramcontent.com/pod-product-compliance
Lightning Source LLC
Chambersburg PA
CBHW030736230426
43667CB00007B/735